GREATEST SPORTS MOMENTS

LAKE PLACID
MIRACLE

WHEN U.S. HOCKEY
STUNNED THE WORLD

BY BLAKE HOENA

ILLUSTRATED BY EDUARDO GARCIA AND RED WOLF STUDIO

CONSULTANT:
BRUCE BERGLUND
PROFESSOR OF HISTORY, CALVIN COLLEGE
GRAND RAPIDS, MICHIGAN

CAPSTONE PRESS
a capstone imprint

Graphic Library is published by Capstone Press,
1710 Roe Crest Drive, North Mankato, Minnesota 56003
www.mycapstone.com

Library of Congress Cataloging-in-Publication data
Names: Hoena, B. A., author. | Garcia, Eduardo, 1970 August 31- illustrator.
Title: Lake Placid miracle : when U. S. hockey stunned the world / by Blake Hoena ; illustrated by Eduardo Garcia.
Other titles: 1980 US hockey team. | 1980 United States hockey team.
Description: North Mankato, Minnesota : Graphic Library, an imprint of Capstone Press, [2018] | Series: Graphic Library. Greatest Sports Moments | Includes index. | Audience: Ages: 8–14.
Identifiers: LCCN 2018001971 (print) | LCCN 2018007830 (ebook) | ISBN 9781543528756 (eBook PDF) | ISBN 9781543528671 (hardcover) | ISBN 9781543528718 (paperback)
Subjects: LCSH: Hockey—United States—History—20th century—Juvenile literature. | Olympic Winter Games (13th : 1980 : Lake Placid, N.Y.)—Juvenile literature. | Hockey teams—United States—Juvenile literature.
Classification: LCC GV848.4.U6 (ebook) | LCC GV848.4.U6 H87 2018 (print) | DDC 796.98—dc23
LC record available at https://lccn.loc.gov/2018001971

Summary: Tells the story of the Miracle on Ice game between the U.S. and U.S.S.R. men's Olympic hockey teams at the 1980 Olympic Games at Lake Placid, New York.

EDITOR
Aaron J. Sautter

ART DIRECTOR
Nathan Gassman

DESIGNER
Ted Williams

MEDIA RESEARCHER
Eric Gohl

PRODUCTION SPECIALIST
Laura Manthe

Direct quotations appear in ***bold italicized text*** on the following pages:

Page 4 (panel 4): from "July 20, 1969: One Giant Leap For Mankind," by NASA, July 20, 2017 (https://www.nasa.gov/mission_pages/apollo/apollo11.html).
Page 6 (panel 2), page 14 (panel 1): from "Spongecoach's Best Herb Brooks Quotes: 29 Inspiring Herb Brooks Quotes to Motivate You," by Spongecoach, September 13, 2017 (http://www.spongecoach.com/inspiring-herb-brooks-quotes/).
Page 25: from "'Do You Believe in Miracles? YES!' ... We Did During USA Hockey Team's Run to Gold Medal" by Steven Marcus, Newsday, February 22, 2015 (https://www.newsday.com/sports/hockey/do-you-believe-in-miracles-yes-we-did-during-usa-hockey-team-s-run-to-gold-medal-1.9963102).
Page 26 (panel 2): from Herb Brooks: Gold Medal Game (http://herbbrooks1980.weebly.com/gold-medal-game.html).

Printed in the United States 4234

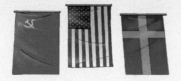

TABLE OF CONTENTS

THE COLD WAR

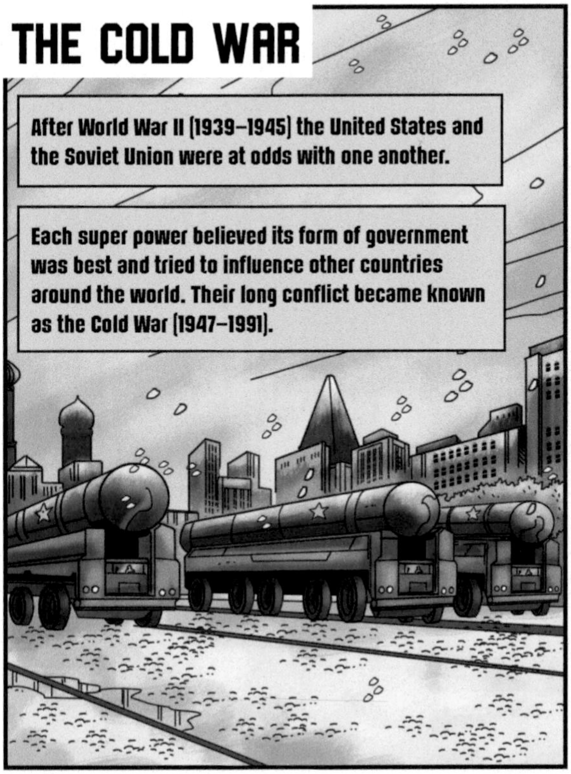
After World War II (1939–1945) the United States and the Soviet Union were at odds with one another.
Each super power believed its form of government was best and tried to influence other countries around the world. Their long conflict became known as the Cold War (1947–1991).

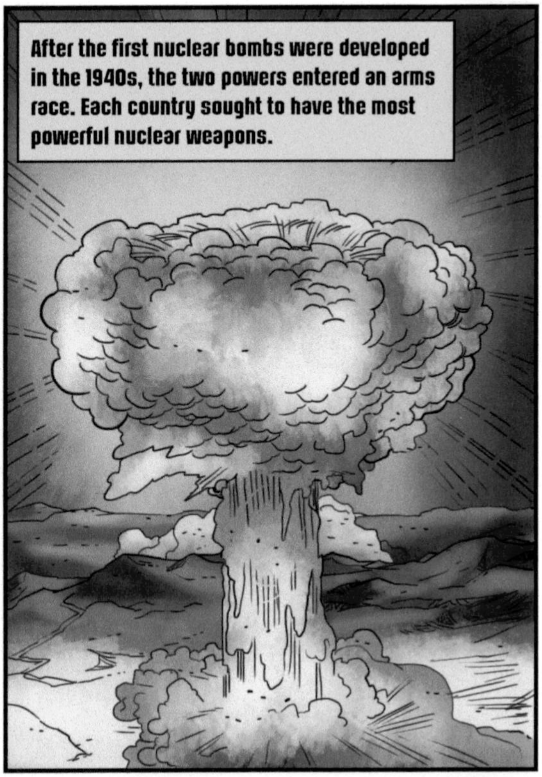
After the first nuclear bombs were developed in the 1940s, the two powers entered an arms race. Each country sought to have the most powerful nuclear weapons.

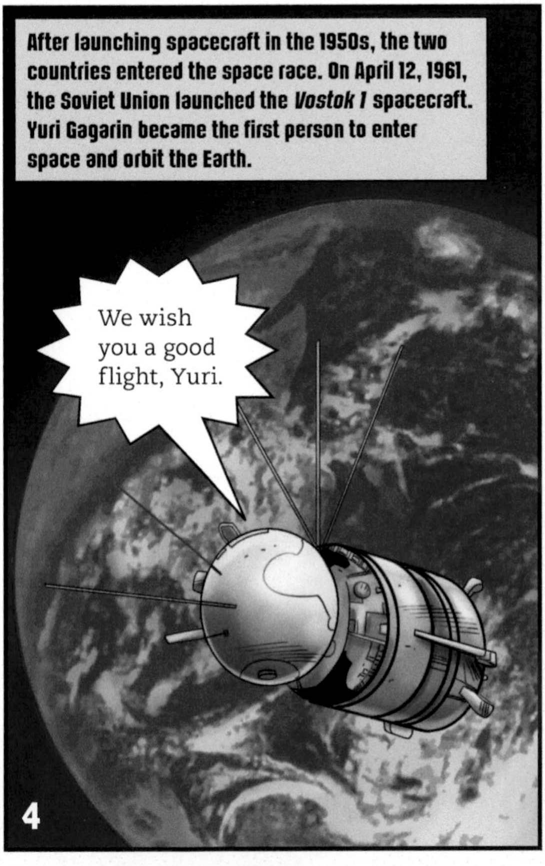
After launching spacecraft in the 1950s, the two countries entered the space race. On April 12, 1961, the Soviet Union launched the *Vostok 1* spacecraft. Yuri Gagarin became the first person to enter space and orbit the Earth.
We wish you a good flight, Yuri.

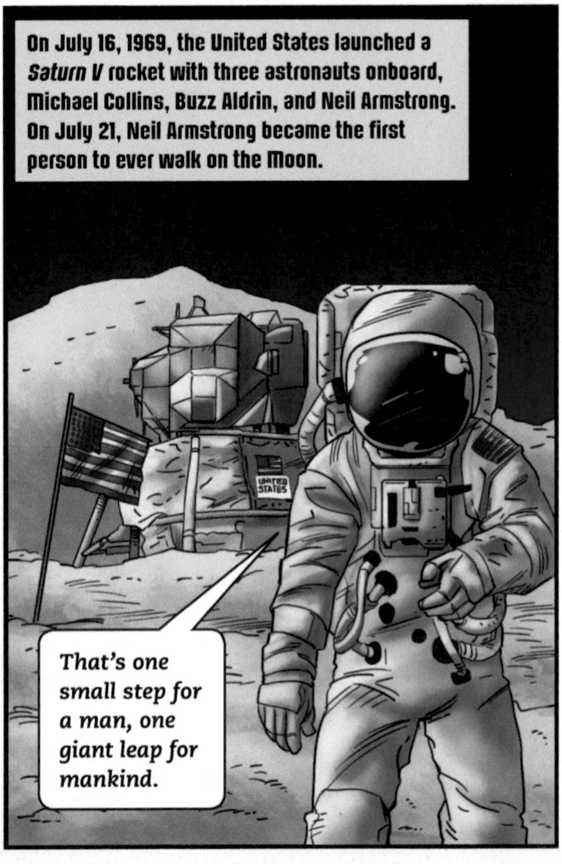
On July 16, 1969, the United States launched a *Saturn V* rocket with three astronauts onboard, Michael Collins, Buzz Aldrin, and Neil Armstrong. On July 21, Neil Armstrong became the first person to ever walk on the Moon.
UNITED STATES
That's one small step for a man, one giant leap for mankind.

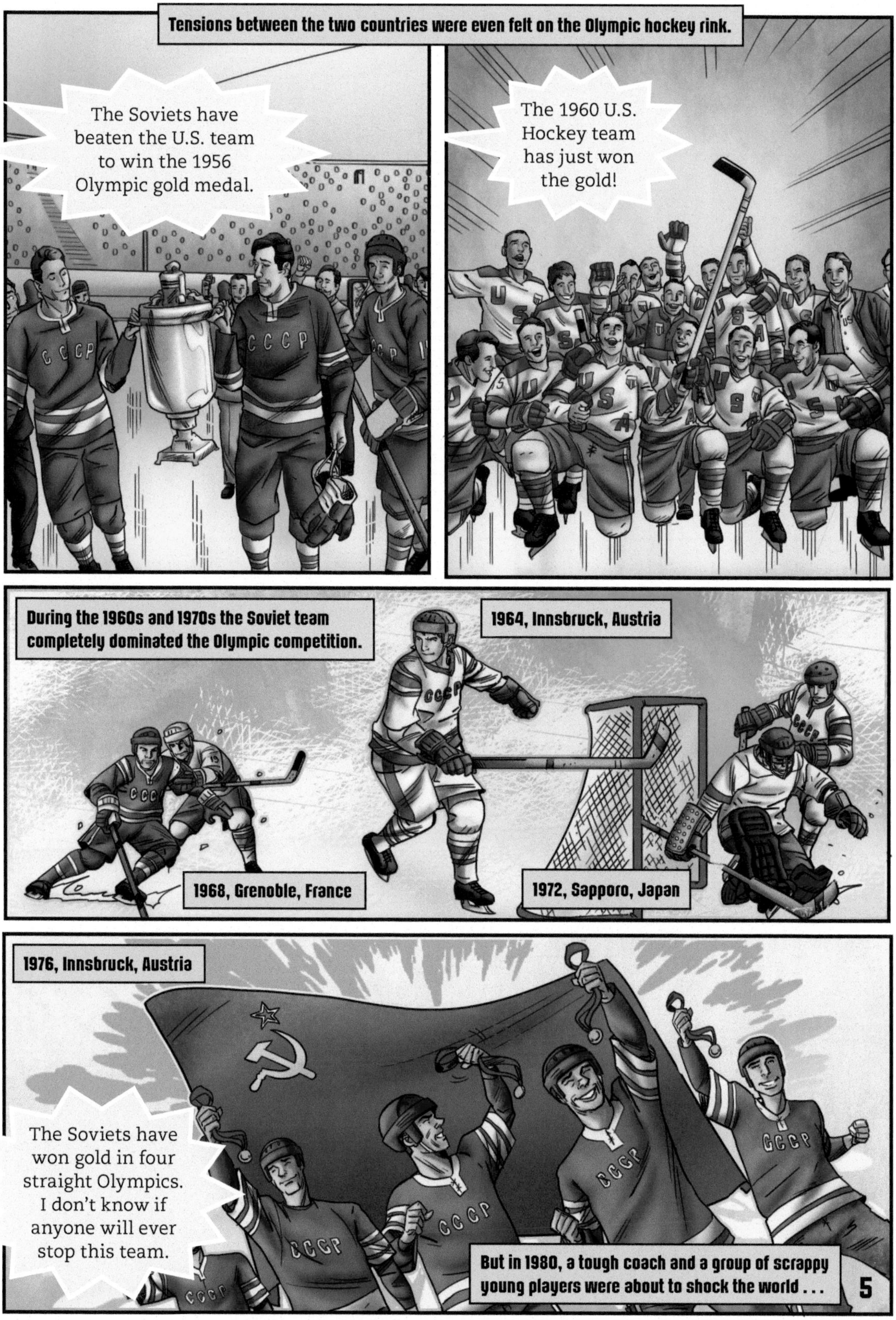
Tensions between the two countries were even felt on the Olympic hockey rink.
The Soviets have beaten the U.S. team to win the 1956 Olympic gold medal.
CCCP
The 1960 U.S. Hockey team has just won the gold!
USA
During the 1960s and 1970s the Soviet team completely dominated the Olympic competition.
1964, Innsbruck, Austria
1968, Grenoble, France
1972, Sapporo, Japan
1976, Innsbruck, Austria
The Soviets have won gold in four straight Olympics. I don't know if anyone will ever stop this team.
CCCP
But in 1980, a tough coach and a group of scrappy young players were about to shock the world . . .

BUILDING A TEAM

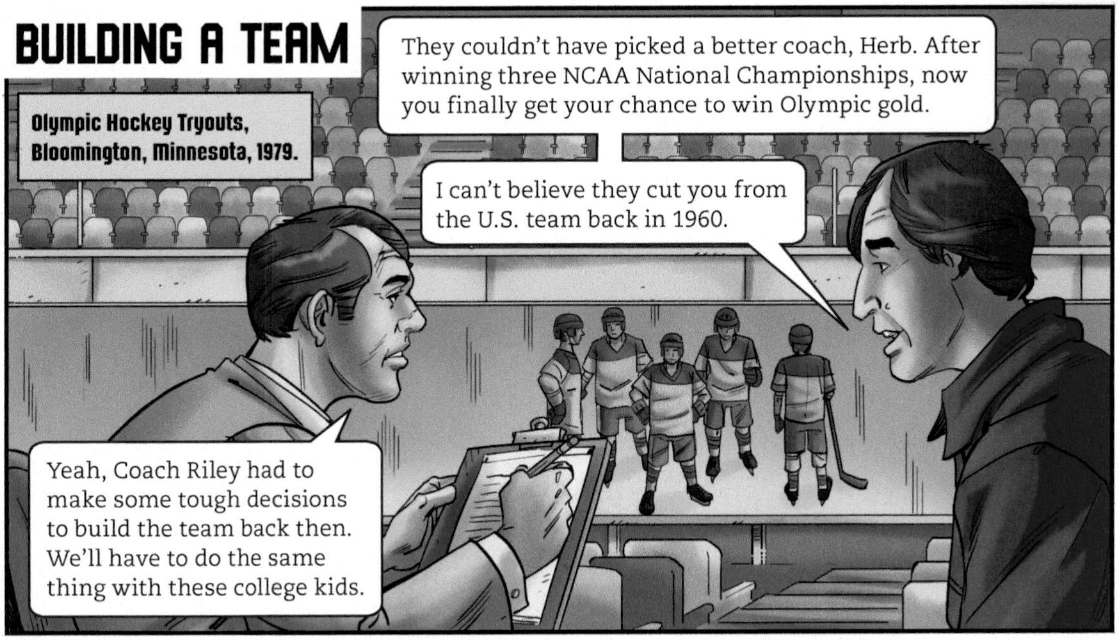

Olympic Hockey Tryouts, Bloomington, Minnesota, 1979.
They couldn't have picked a better coach, Herb. After winning three NCAA National Championships, now you finally get your chance to win Olympic gold.
I can't believe they cut you from the U.S. team back in 1960.
Yeah, Coach Riley had to make some tough decisions to build the team back then. We'll have to do the same thing with these college kids.

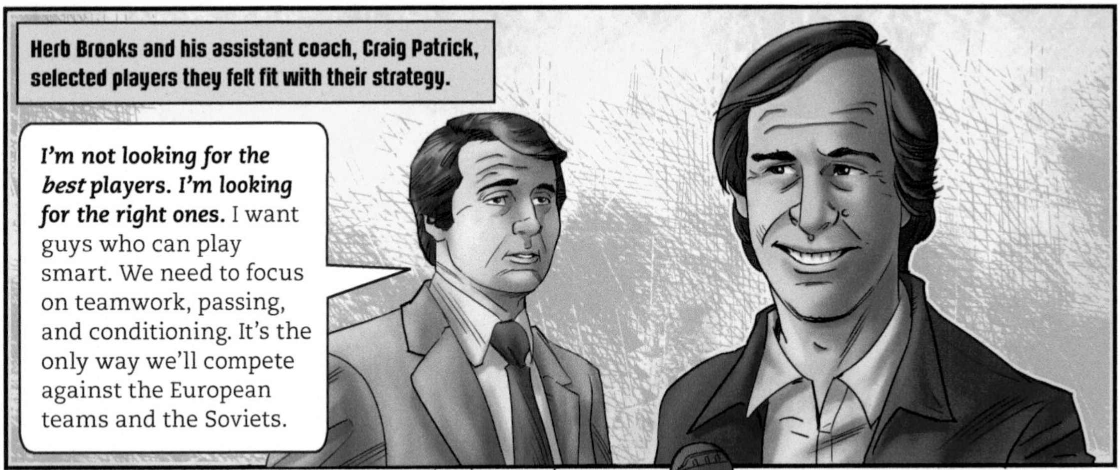

Herb Brooks and his assistant coach, Craig Patrick, selected players they felt fit with their strategy.
I'm not looking for the best players. I'm looking for the right ones. I want guys who can play smart. We need to focus on teamwork, passing, and conditioning. It's the only way we'll compete against the European teams and the Soviets.

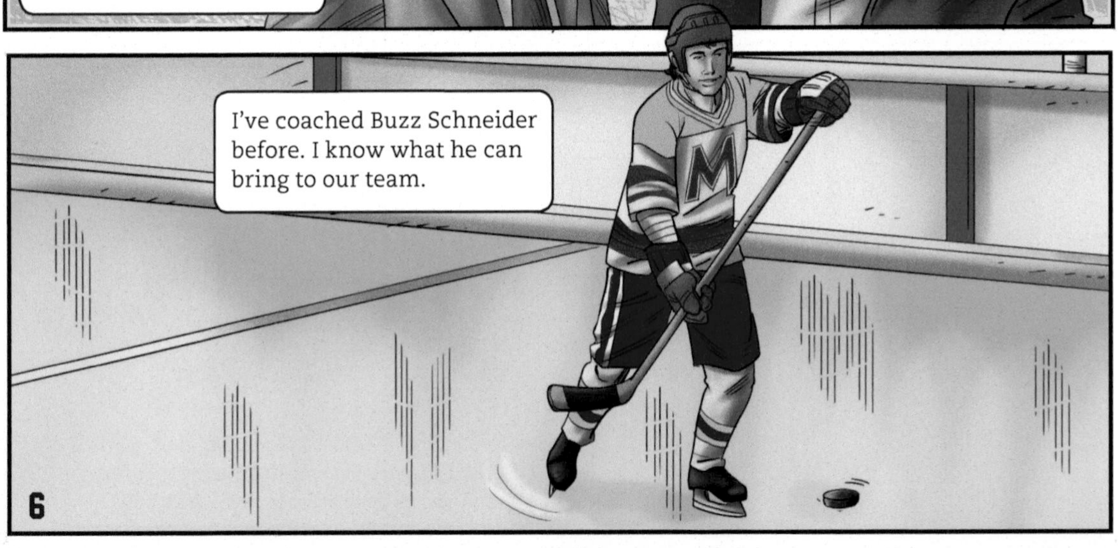

I've coached Buzz Schneider before. I know what he can bring to our team.

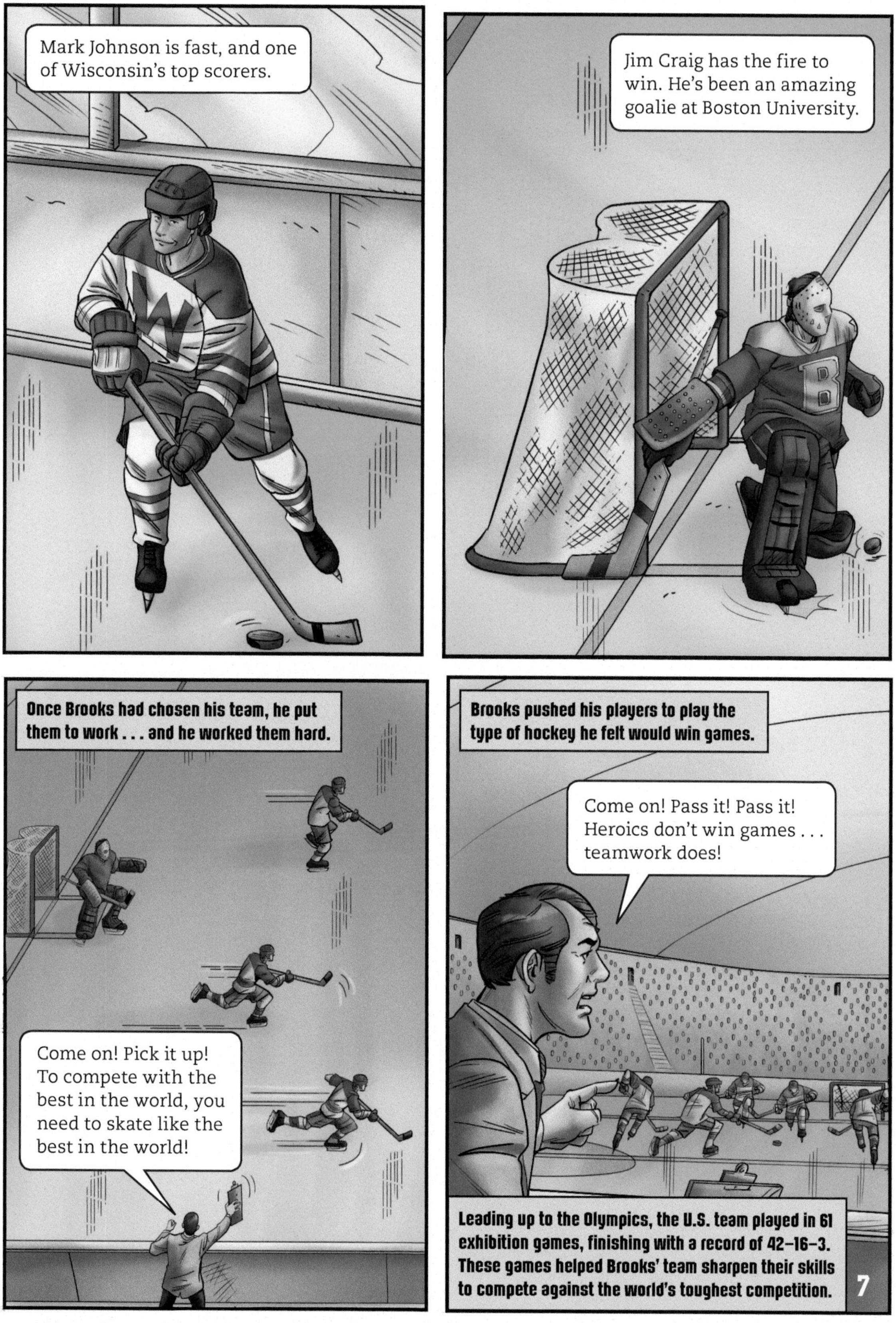
Mark Johnson is fast, and one of Wisconsin's top scorers.
Jim Craig has the fire to win. He's been an amazing goalie at Boston University.
Once Brooks had chosen his team, he put them to work . . . and he worked them hard.
Come on! Pick it up! To compete with the best in the world, you need to skate like the best in the world!
Brooks pushed his players to play the type of hockey he felt would win games.
Come on! Pass it! Pass it! Heroics don't win games . . . teamwork does!
Leading up to the Olympics, the U.S. team played in 61 exhibition games, finishing with a record of 42–16–3. These games helped Brooks' team sharpen their skills to compete against the world's toughest competition.

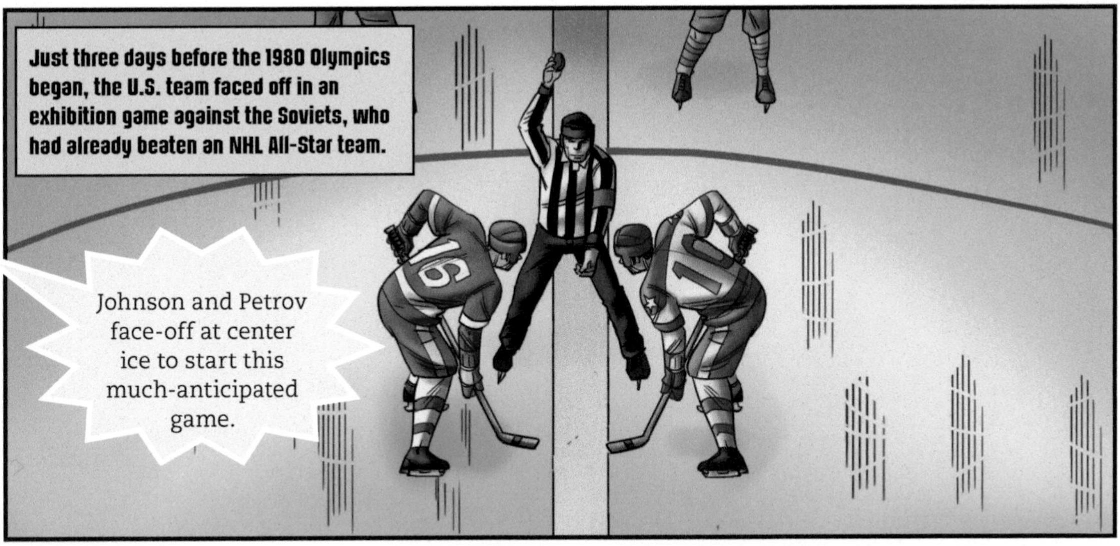
Just three days before the 1980 Olympics began, the U.S. team faced off in an exhibition game against the Soviets, who had already beaten an NHL All-Star team.
Johnson and Petrov face-off at center ice to start this much-anticipated game.

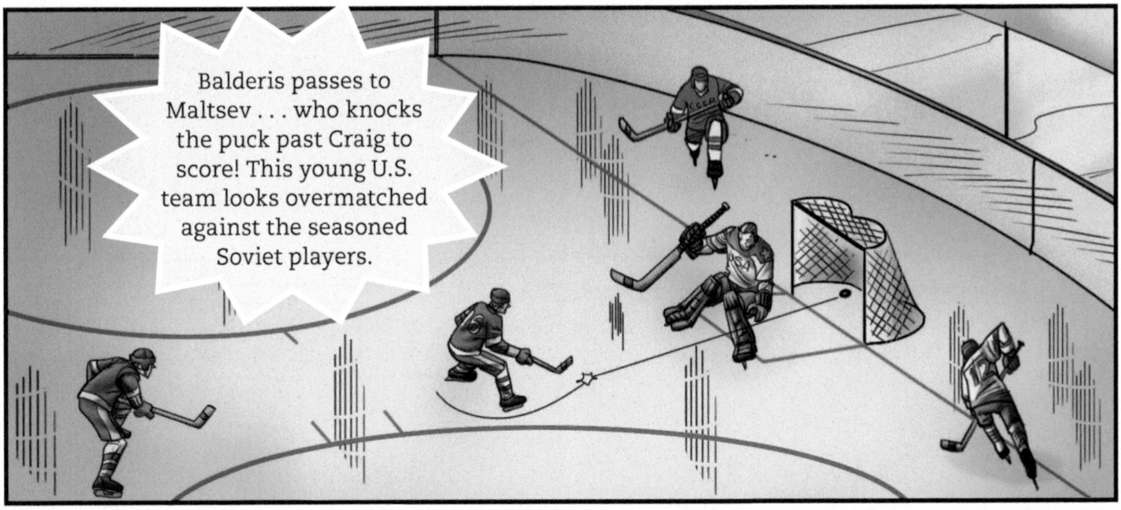
Balderis passes to Maltsev . . . who knocks the puck past Craig to score! This young U.S. team looks overmatched against the seasoned Soviet players.

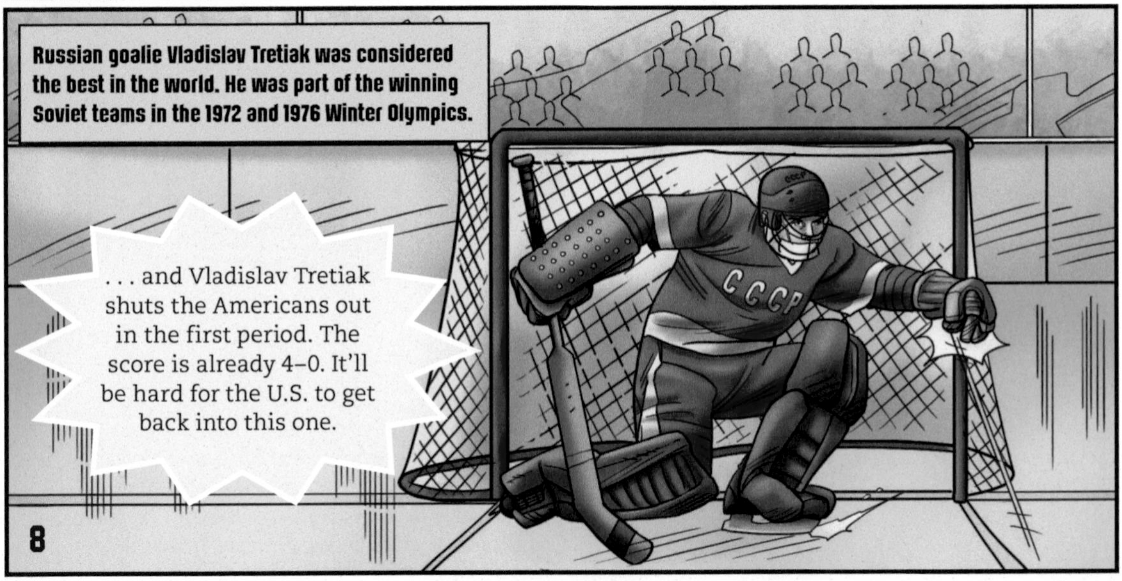
Russian goalie Vladislav Tretiak was considered the best in the world. He was part of the winning Soviet teams in the 1972 and 1976 Winter Olympics.
. . . and Vladislav Tretiak shuts the Americans out in the first period. The score is already 4–0. It'll be hard for the U.S. to get back into this one.

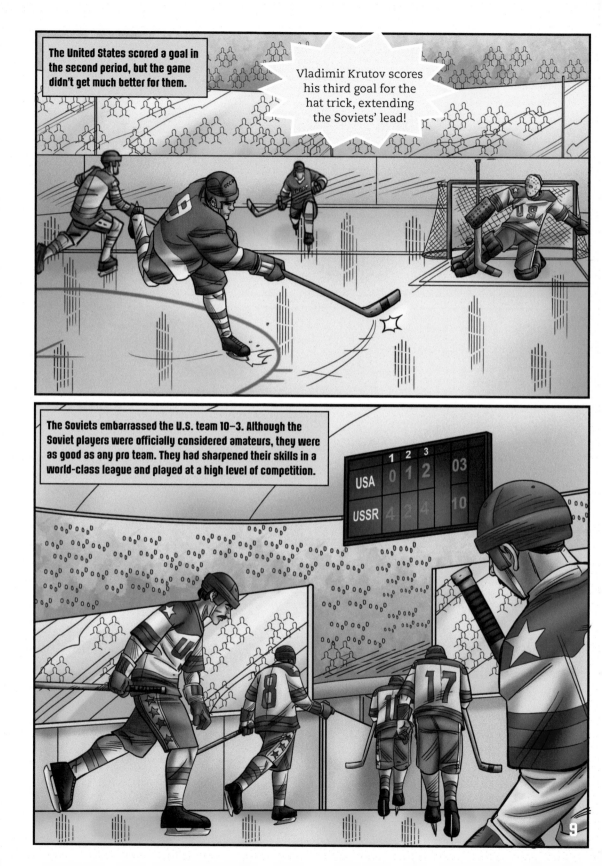

The United States scored a goal in the second period, but the game didn't get much better for them.

Vladimir Krutov scores his third goal for the hat trick, extending the Soviets' lead!

The Soviets embarrassed the U.S. team 10–3. Although the Soviet players were officially considered amateurs, they were as good as any pro team. They had sharpened their skills in a world-class league and played at a high level of competition.

	1	2	3	
USA	0	1	2	03
USSR	4	2	4	10

GETTING TO THE FINALS

The 1980 Olympic hockey tournament began with group play. Teams played against each team in their division.

Blue Division	Red Division
• Czechoslovakia	• Canada
• Norway	• Finland
• Romania	• Japan
• Sweden	• Netherlands
• West Germany	• Poland
• United States	• Soviet Union

We have to play Sweden first. And then Czechoslovakia. Both are serious medal contenders.

We have a tough draw, but I believe we can finish in the top two in our division. That'll get us to the medal round.

February 12, 1980. U.S.A. vs. Sweden.

. . . Berglund has the puck and passes to Molin . . .

. . . Molin gives it to Andersson, who takes a shot and scores! Team Sweden gets on the board first.

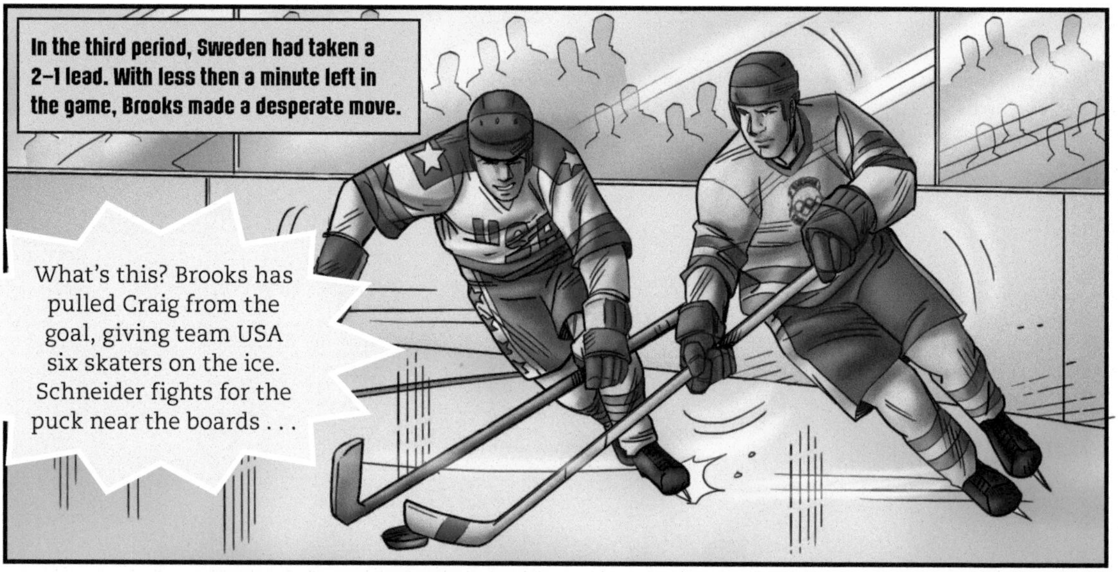
In the third period, Sweden had taken a 2–1 lead. With less then a minute left in the game, Brooks made a desperate move.
What's this? Brooks has pulled Craig from the goal, giving team USA six skaters on the ice. Schneider fights for the puck near the boards . . .

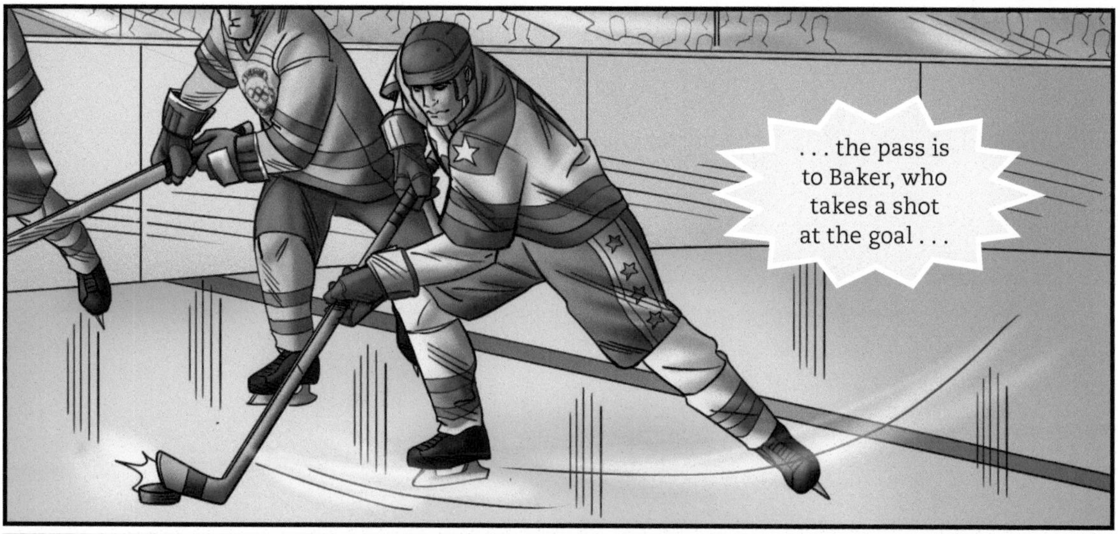
. . . the pass is to Baker, who takes a shot at the goal . . .

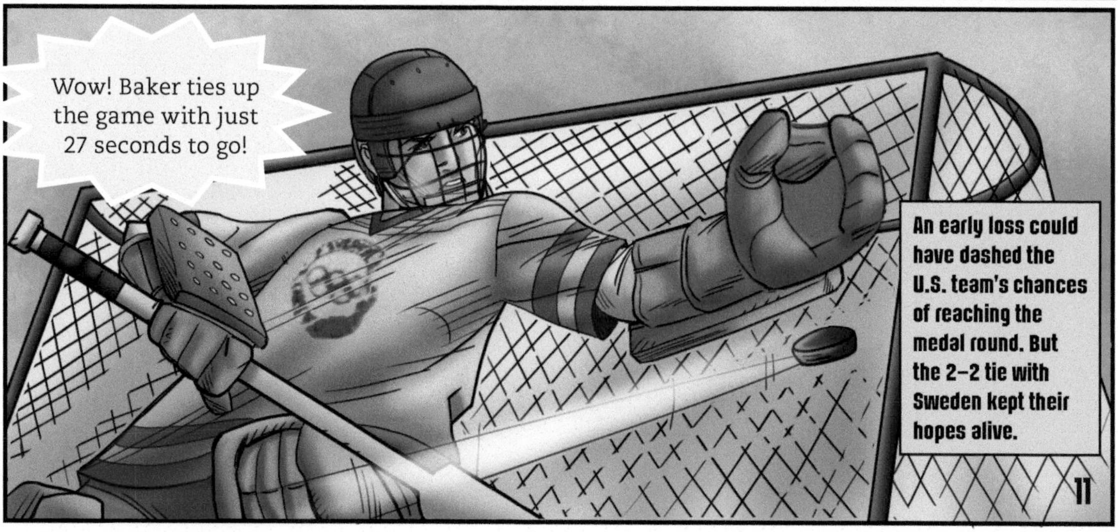
Wow! Baker ties up the game with just 27 seconds to go!
An early loss could have dashed the U.S. team's chances of reaching the medal round. But the 2–2 tie with Sweden kept their hopes alive.

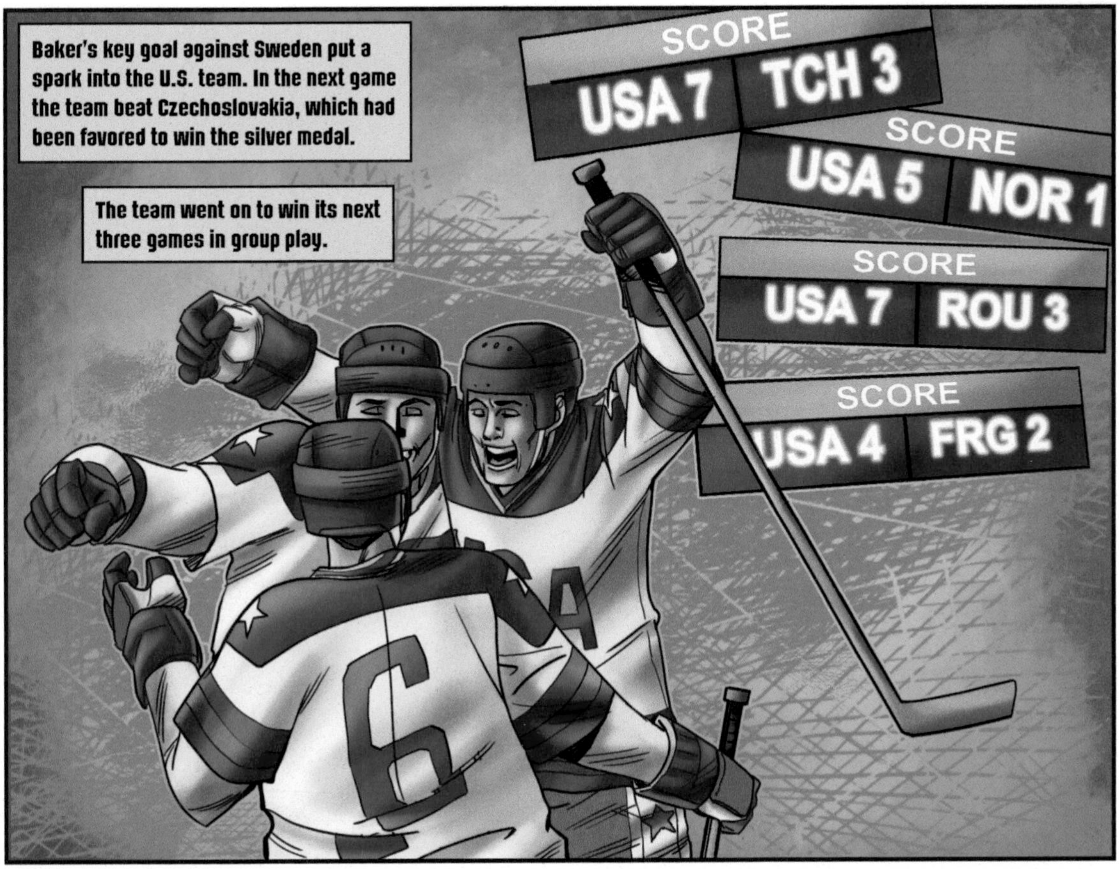
Baker's key goal against Sweden put a spark into the U.S. team. In the next game the team beat Czechoslovakia, which had been favored to win the silver medal.
The team went on to win its next three games in group play.
SCORE
USA 7 TCH 3
SCORE
USA 5 NOR 1
SCORE
USA 7 ROU 3
SCORE
USA 4 FRG 2

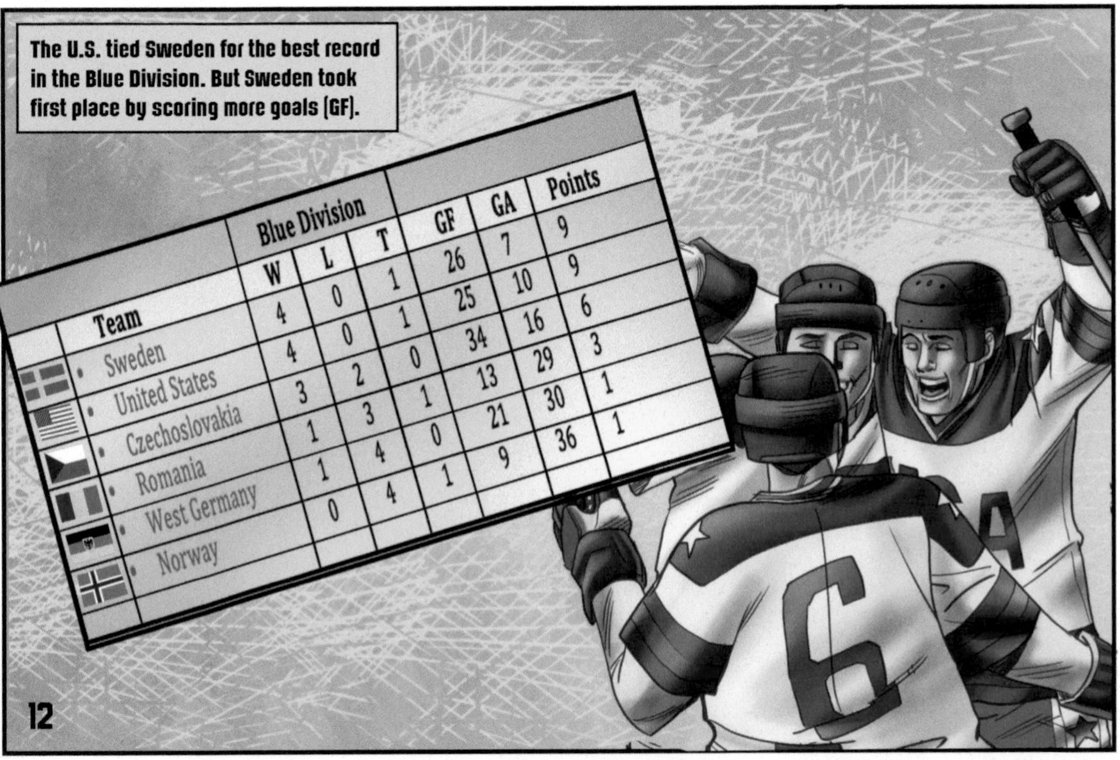
The U.S. tied Sweden for the best record in the Blue Division. But Sweden took first place by scoring more goals (GF).

Team	Blue Division W	L	T	GF	GA	Points
Sweden	4	0	1	26	7	9
United States	4	0	1	25	10	9
Czechoslovakia	3	2	0	34	16	6
Romania	1	3	1	13	29	3
West Germany	1	4	0	21	30	1
Norway	0	4	1	9	36	1

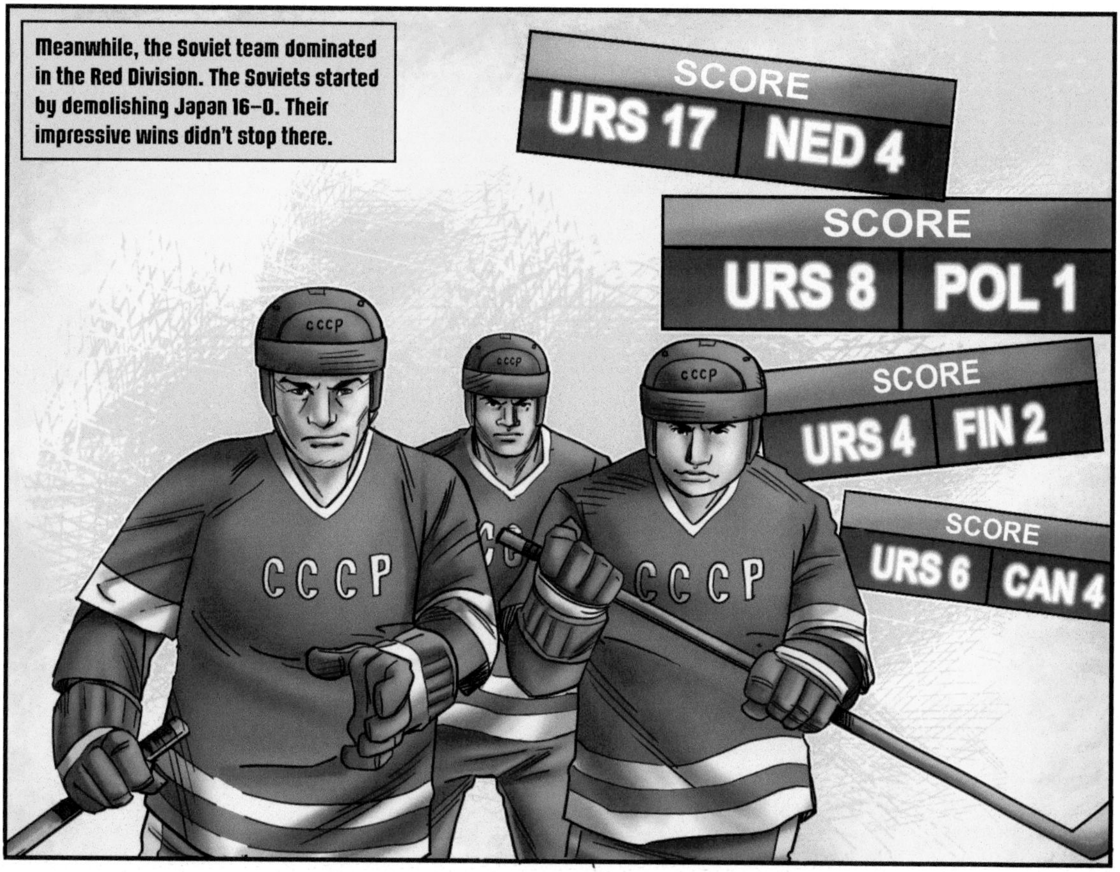
Meanwhile, the Soviet team dominated in the Red Division. The Soviets started by demolishing Japan 16–0. Their impressive wins didn't stop there.
SCORE
URS 17
NED 4
SCORE
URS 8
POL 1
SCORE
URS 4
FIN 2
SCORE
URS 6
CAN 4
CCCP

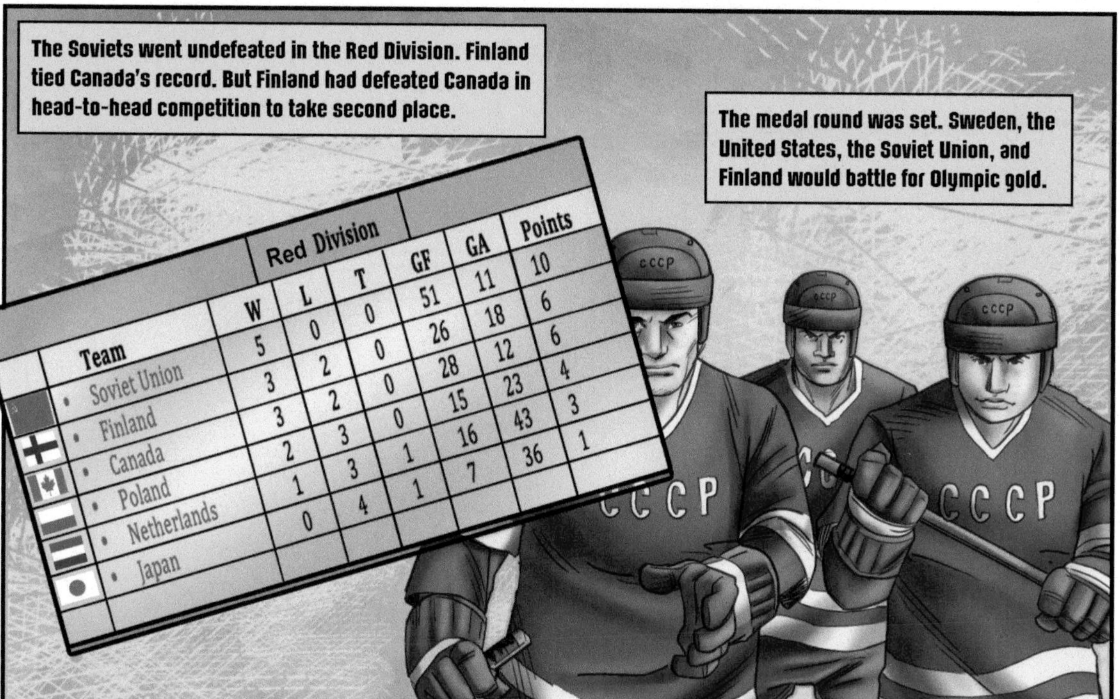
The Soviets went undefeated in the Red Division. Finland tied Canada's record. But Finland had defeated Canada in head-to-head competition to take second place.
The medal round was set. Sweden, the United States, the Soviet Union, and Finland would battle for Olympic gold.
CCCP

Team	Red Division W	L	T	GF	GA	Points
Soviet Union	5	0	0	51	11	10
Finland	3	2	0	26	18	6
Canada	3	2	0	28	12	6
Poland	2	3	0	15	23	4
Netherlands	1	3	1	16	43	3
Japan	0	4	1	7	36	1

THE MIRACLE

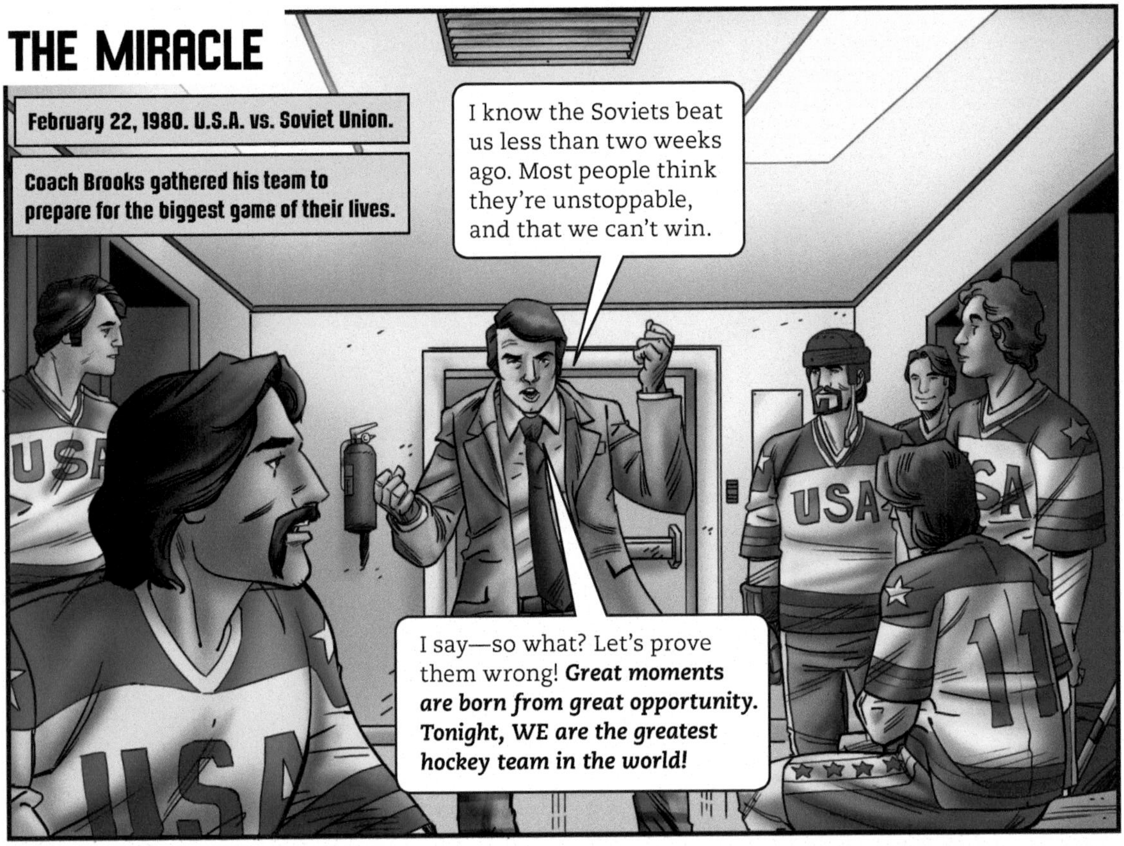
February 22, 1980. U.S.A. vs. Soviet Union.
Coach Brooks gathered his team to prepare for the biggest game of their lives.
I know the Soviets beat us less than two weeks ago. Most people think they're unstoppable, and that we can't win.
I say—so what? Let's prove them wrong! *Great moments are born from great opportunity. Tonight, WE are the greatest hockey team in the world!*

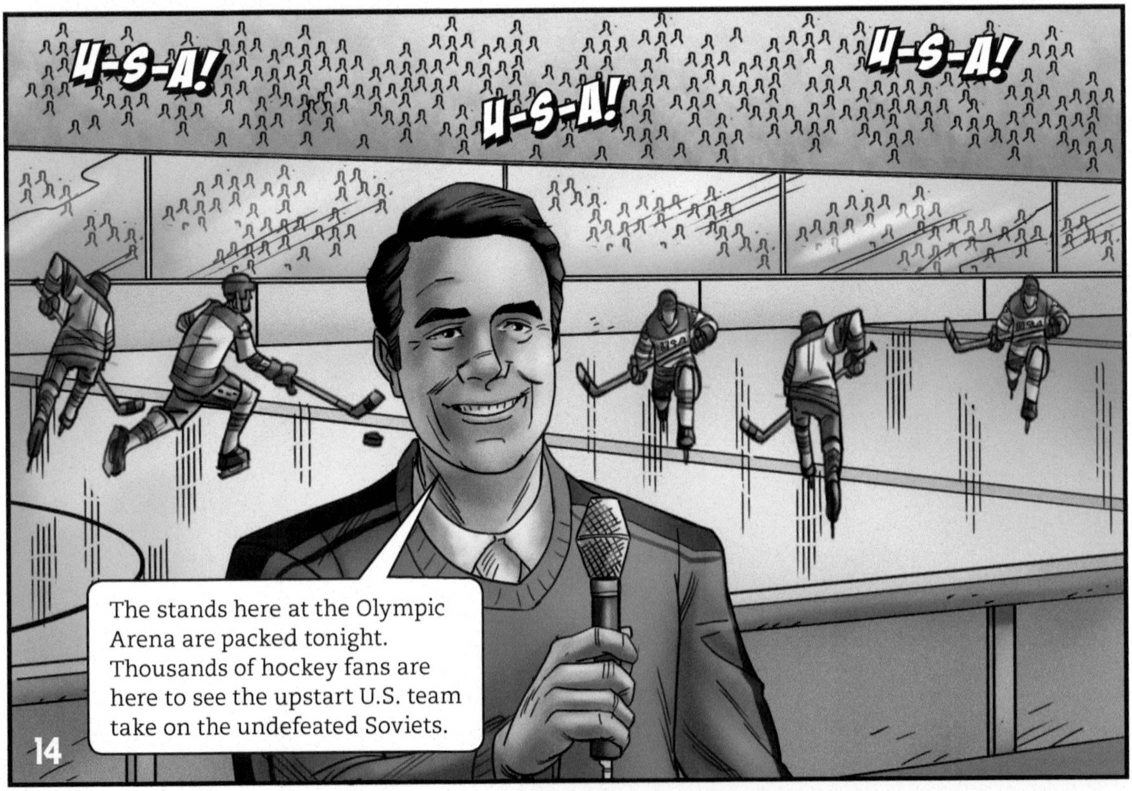
U-S-A!
U-S-A!
U-S-A!
The stands here at the Olympic Arena are packed tonight. Thousands of hockey fans are here to see the upstart U.S. team take on the undefeated Soviets.

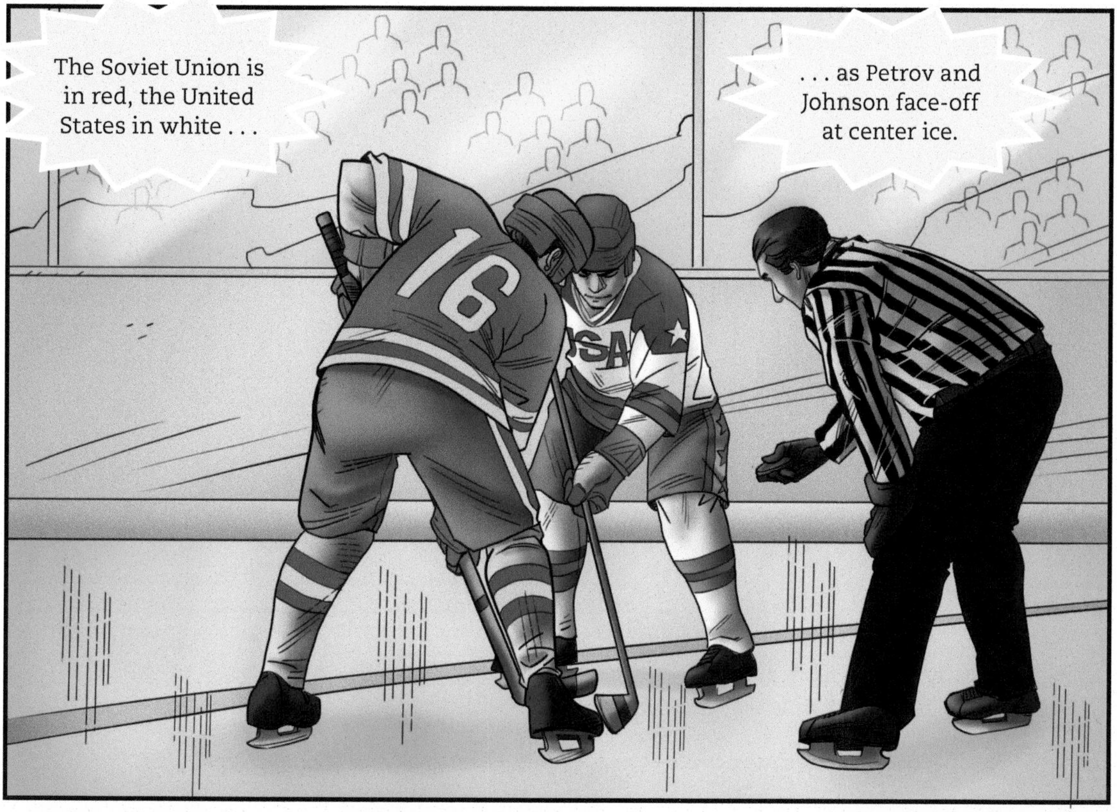
The Soviet Union is in red, the United States in white . . .
. . . as Petrov and Johnson face-off at center ice.
16
USA

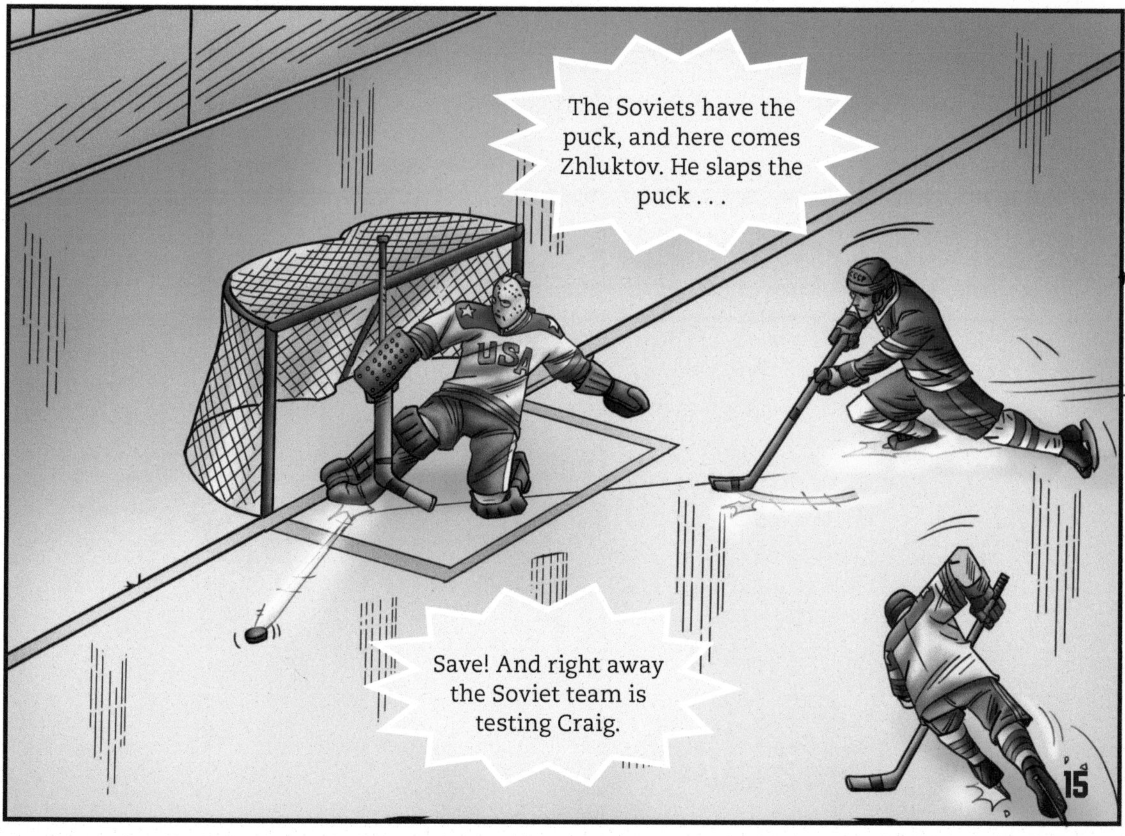
The Soviets have the puck, and here comes Zhluktov. He slaps the puck . . .
USA
Save! And right away the Soviet team is testing Craig.

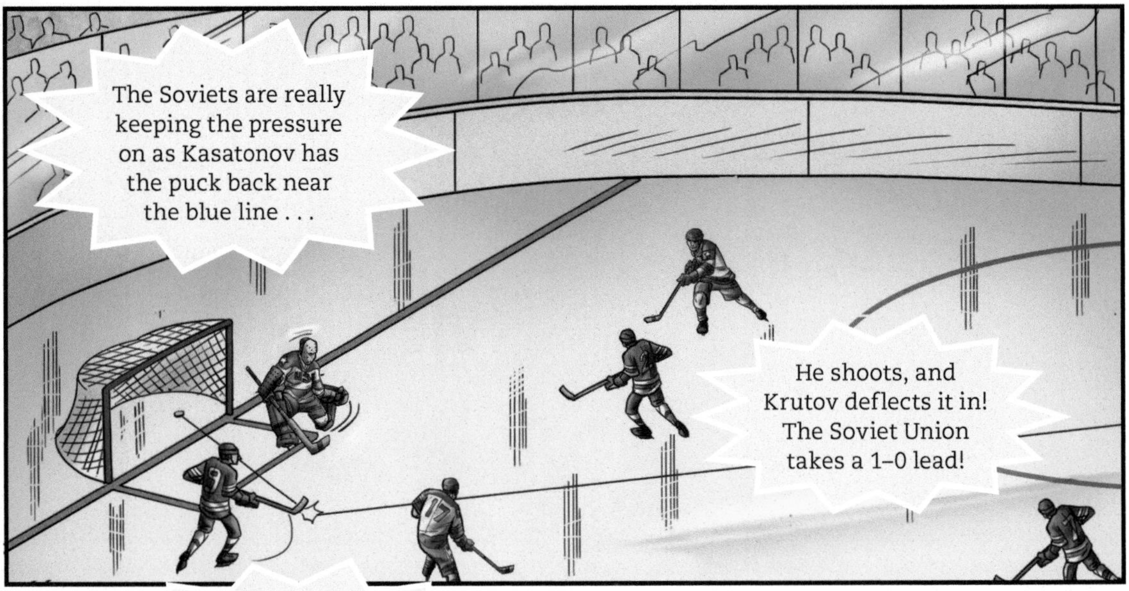
The Soviets are really keeping the pressure on as Kasatonov has the puck back near the blue line . . .
He shoots, and Krutov deflects it in! The Soviet Union takes a 1–0 lead!

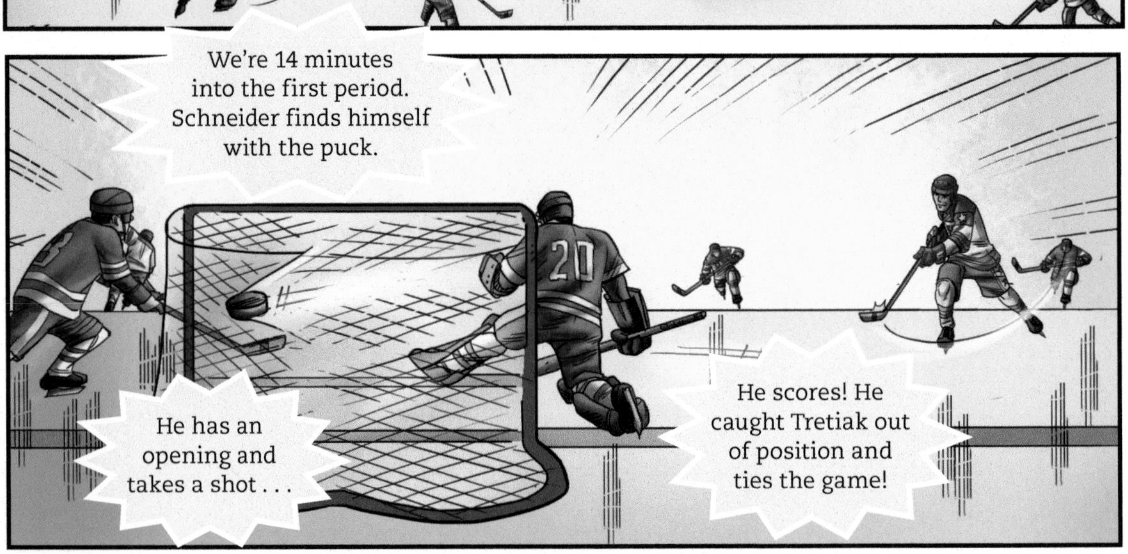
We're 14 minutes into the first period. Schneider finds himself with the puck.
He has an opening and takes a shot . . .
He scores! He caught Tretiak out of position and ties the game!

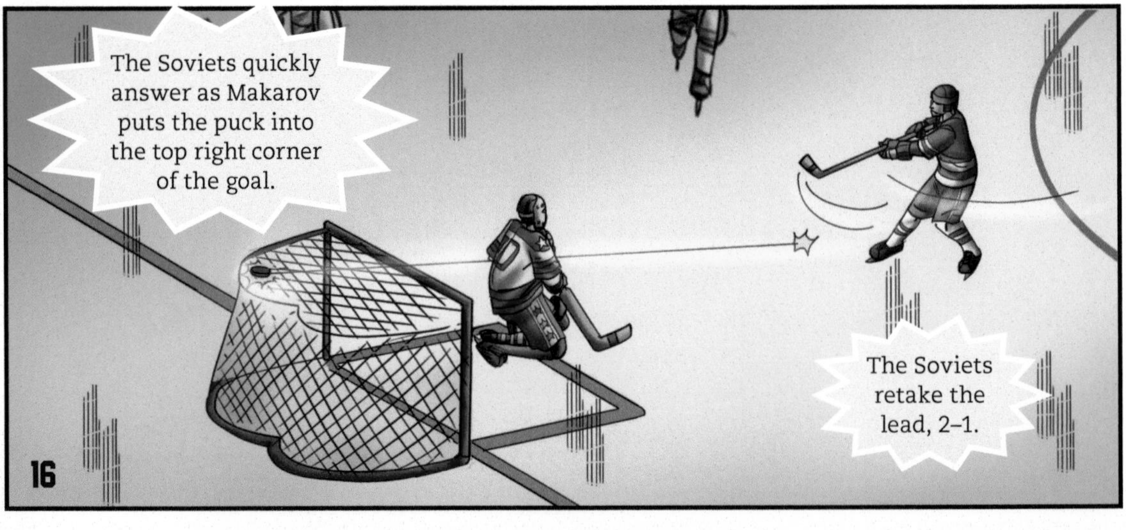
The Soviets quickly answer as Makarov puts the puck into the top right corner of the goal.
The Soviets retake the lead, 2–1.

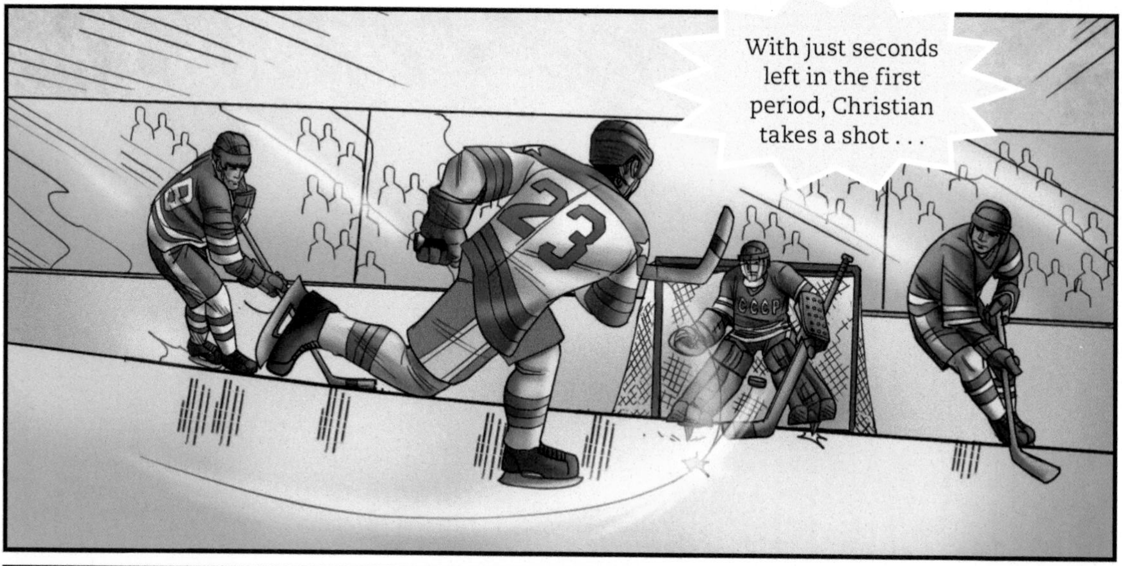
With just seconds left in the first period, Christian takes a shot . . .

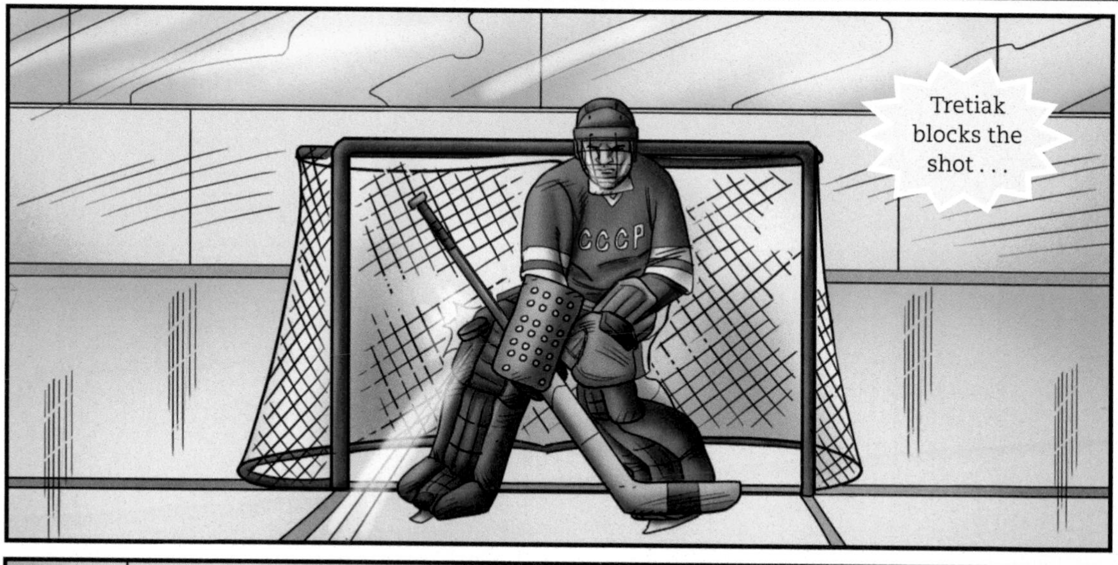
Tretiak blocks the shot . . .

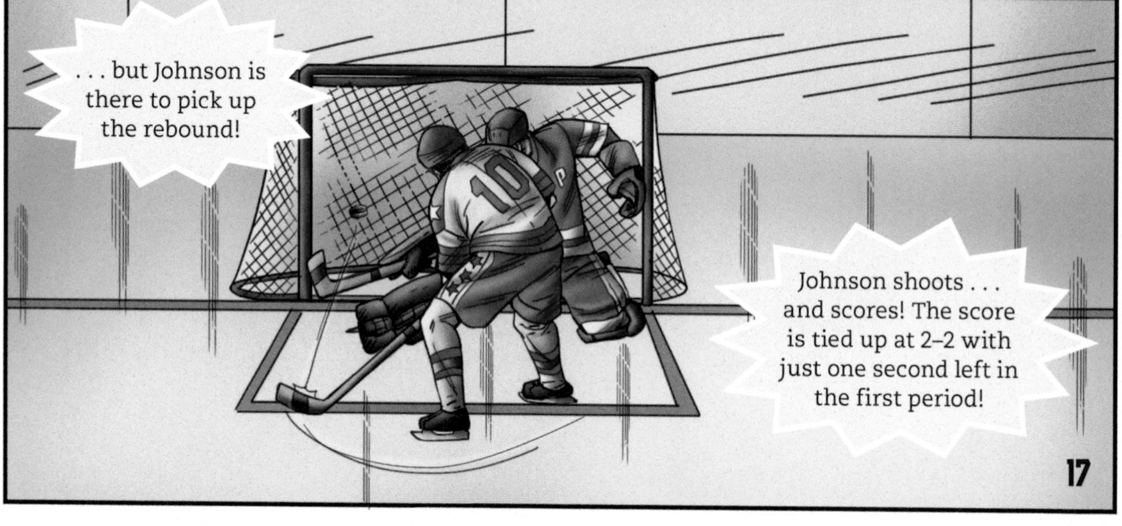
. . . but Johnson is there to pick up the rebound!
Johnson shoots . . . and scores! The score is tied up at 2–2 with just one second left in the first period!

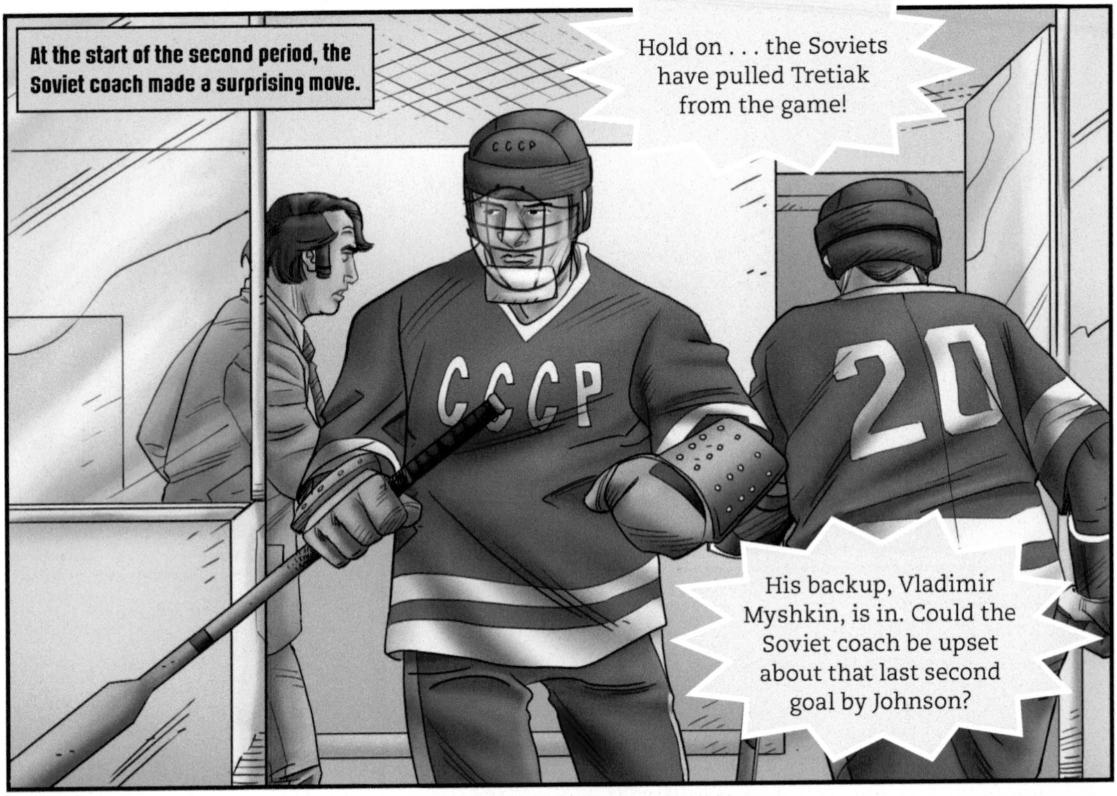
At the start of the second period, the Soviet coach made a surprising move.
Hold on . . . the Soviets have pulled Tretiak from the game!
CCCP
20
His backup, Vladimir Myshkin, is in. Could the Soviet coach be upset about that last second goal by Johnson?

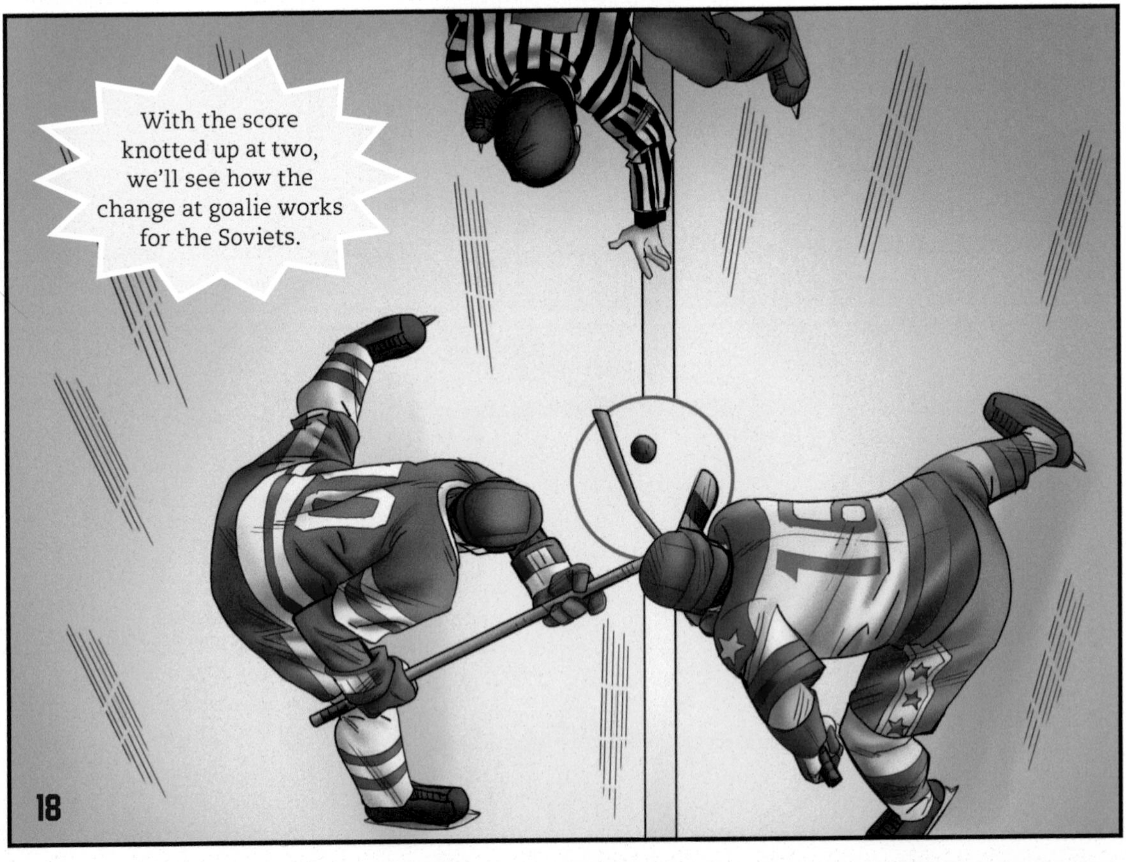
With the score knotted up at two, we'll see how the change at goalie works for the Soviets.

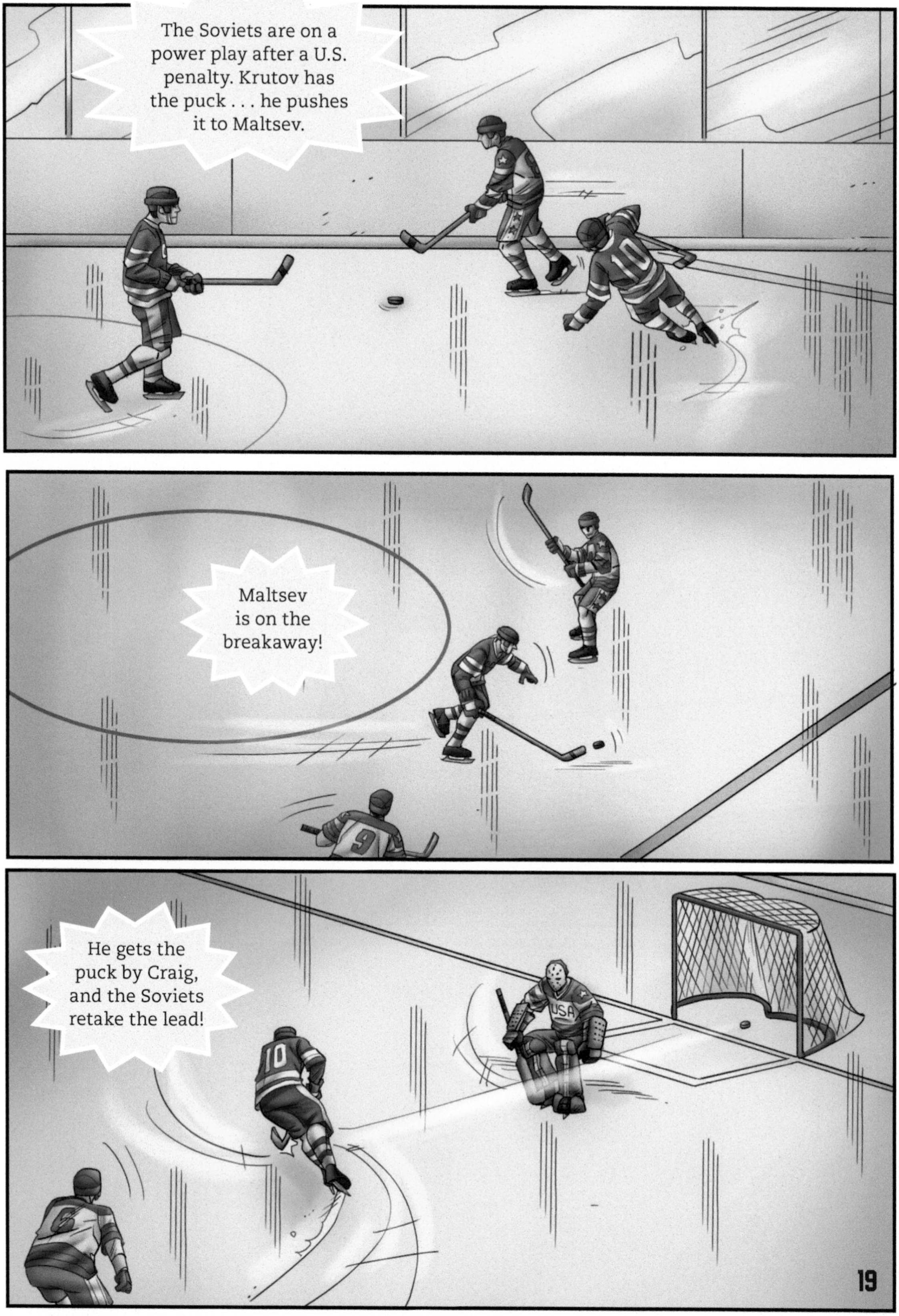
The Soviets are on a power play after a U.S. penalty. Krutov has the puck . . . he pushes it to Maltsev.
10
Maltsev is on the breakaway!
9
He gets the puck by Craig, and the Soviets retake the lead!
USA
10

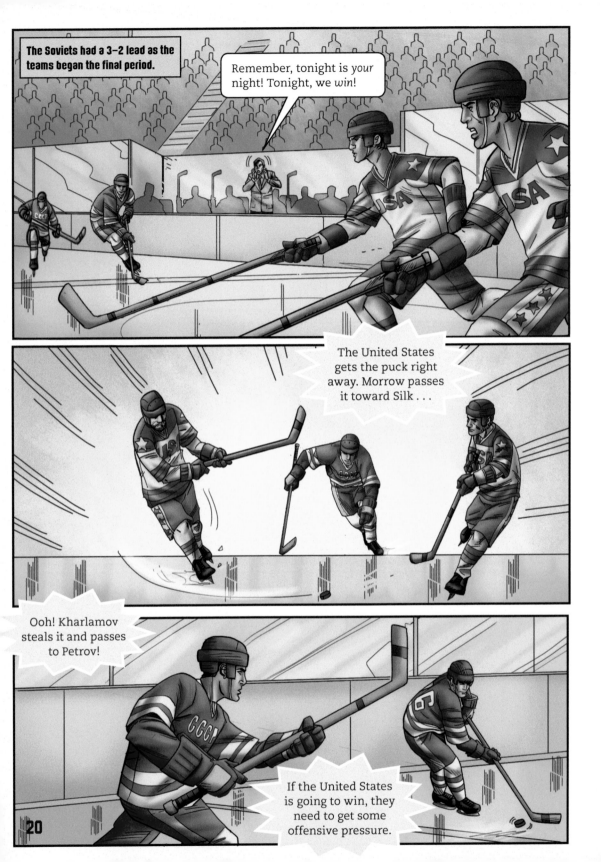

The Soviets had a 3–2 lead as the teams began the final period.

Remember, tonight is *your* night! Tonight, we *win*!

The United States gets the puck right away. Morrow passes it toward Silk . . .

Ooh! Kharlamov steals it and passes to Petrov!

If the United States is going to win, they need to get some offensive pressure.

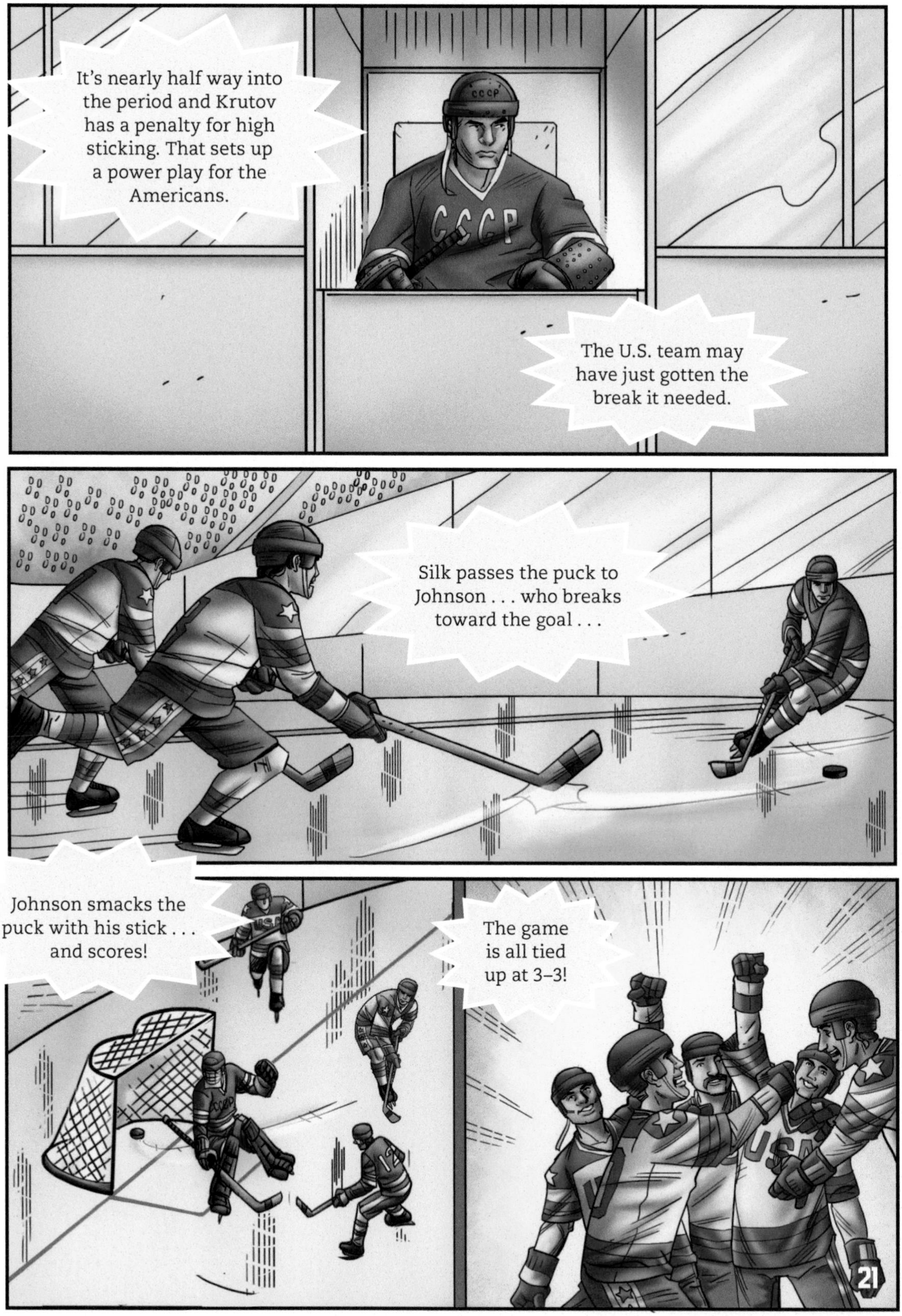
It's nearly half way into the period and Krutov has a penalty for high sticking. That sets up a power play for the Americans.
CCCP
The U.S. team may have just gotten the break it needed.
Silk passes the puck to Johnson . . . who breaks toward the goal . . .
Johnson smacks the puck with his stick . . . and scores!
The game is all tied up at 3–3!

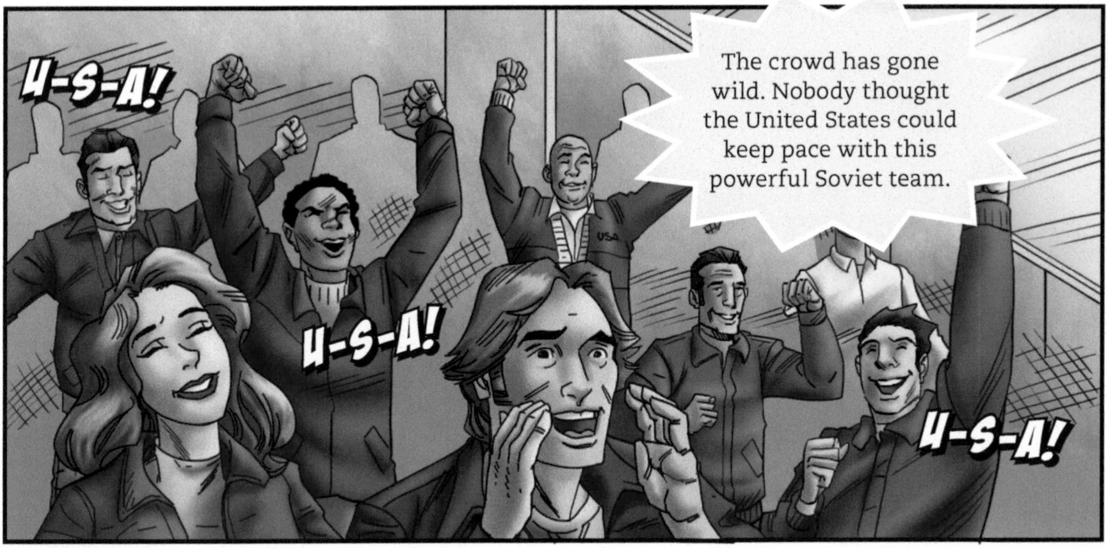
U-S-A!
The crowd has gone wild. Nobody thought the United States could keep pace with this powerful Soviet team.
U-S-A!
U-S-A!

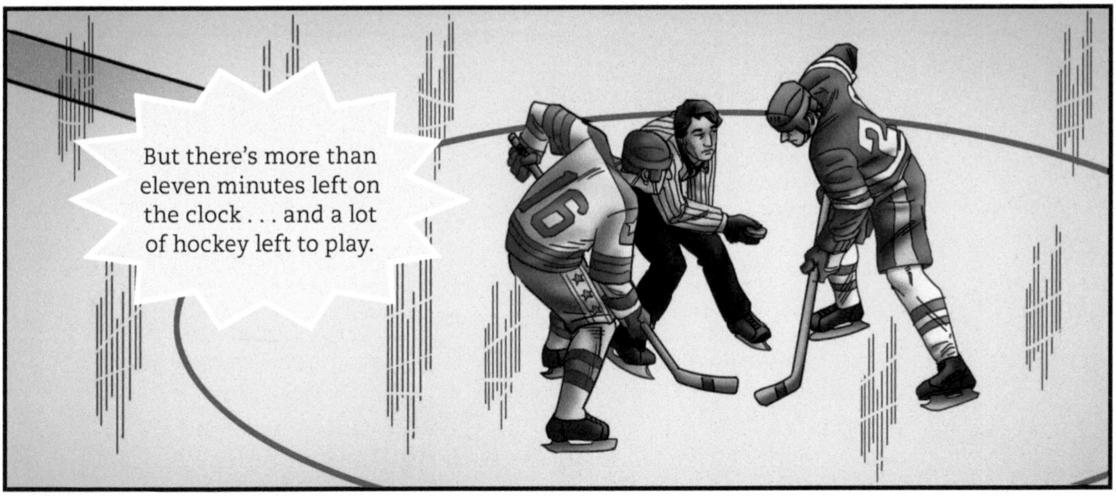
But there's more than eleven minutes left on the clock . . . and a lot of hockey left to play.

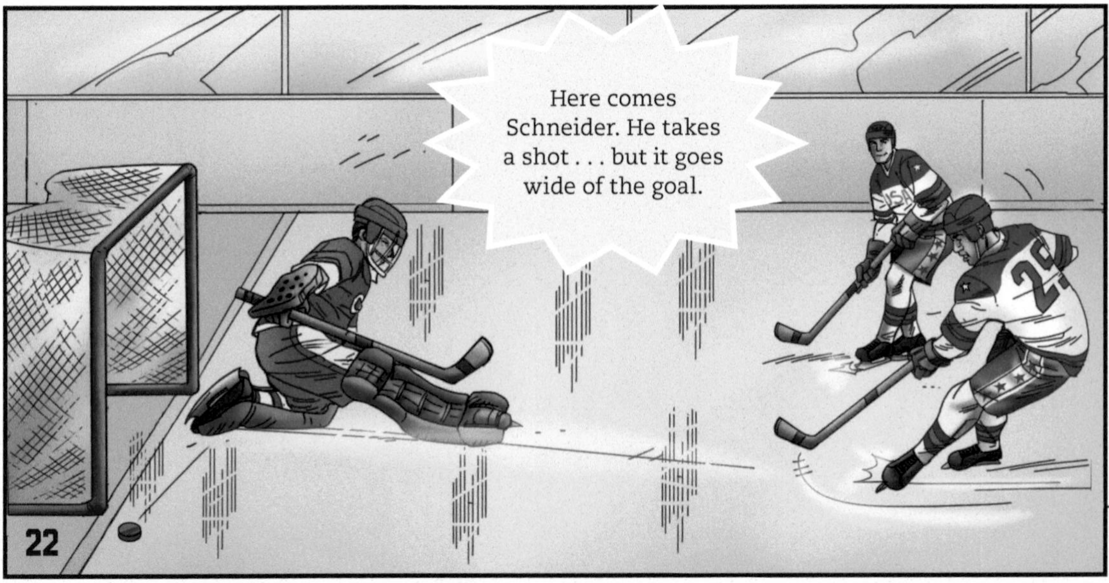
Here comes Schneider. He takes a shot . . . but it goes wide of the goal.

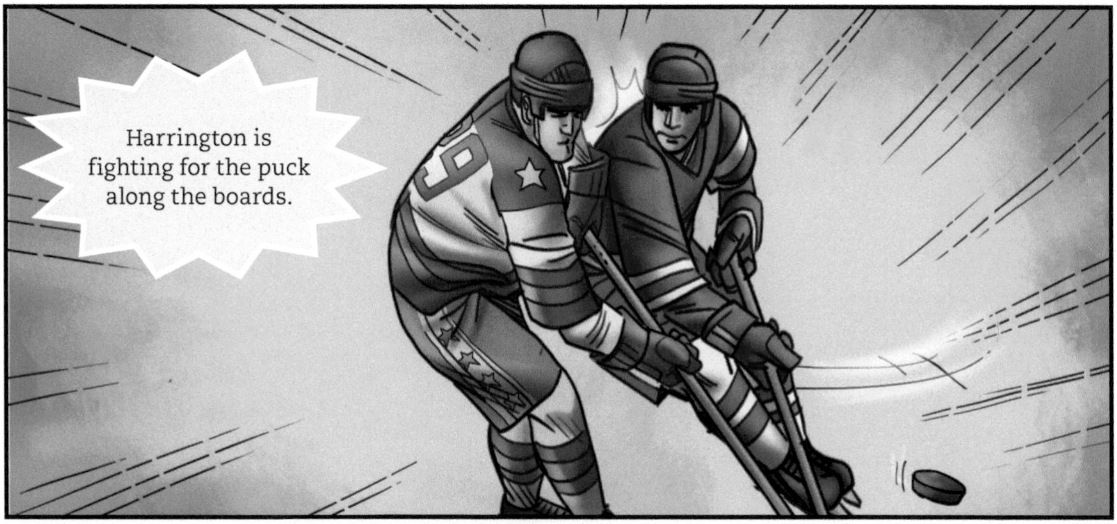
Harrington is fighting for the puck along the boards.

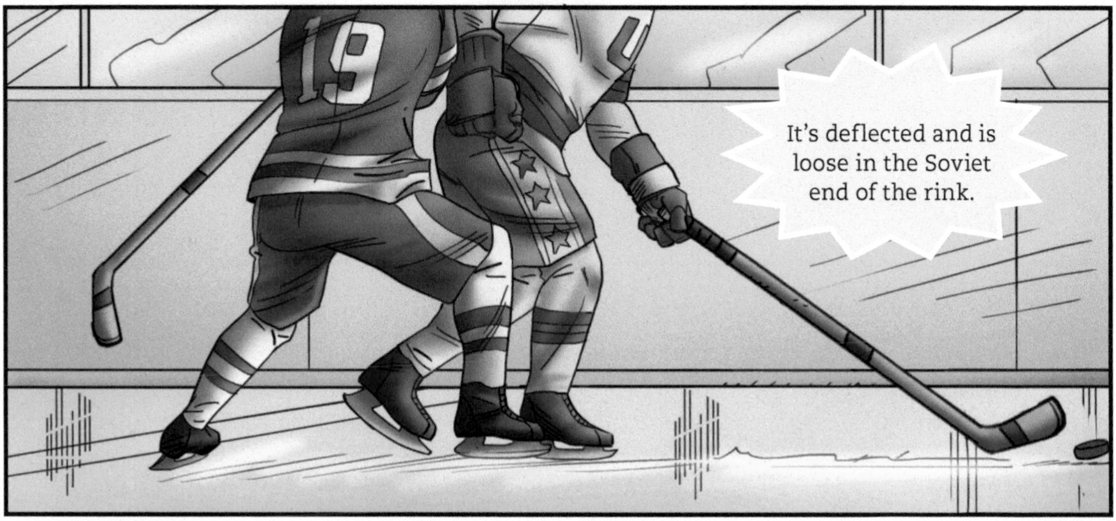
It's deflected and is loose in the Soviet end of the rink.

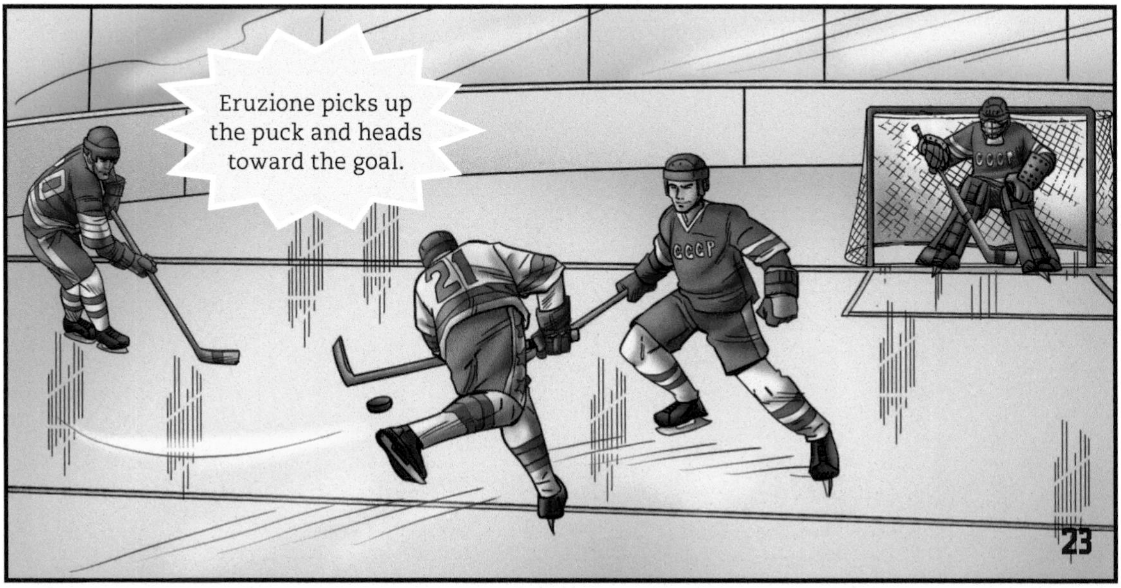
Eruzione picks up the puck and heads toward the goal.

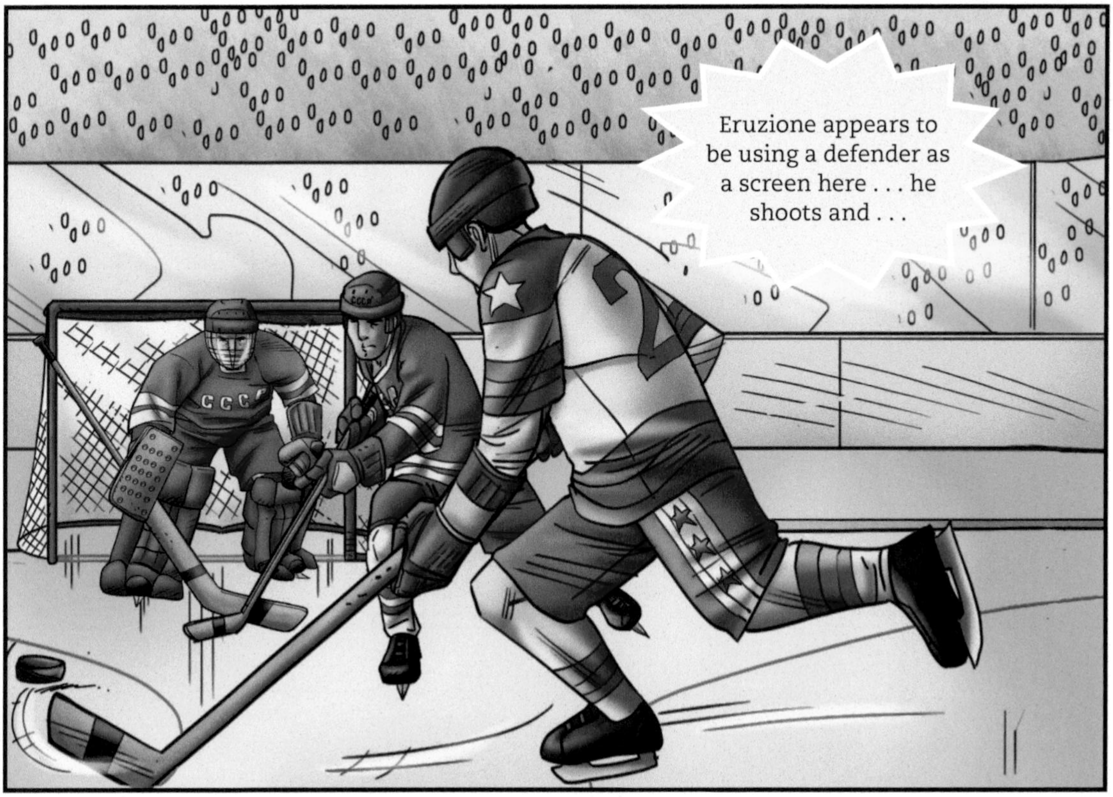
Eruzione appears to be using a defender as a screen here . . . he shoots and . . .

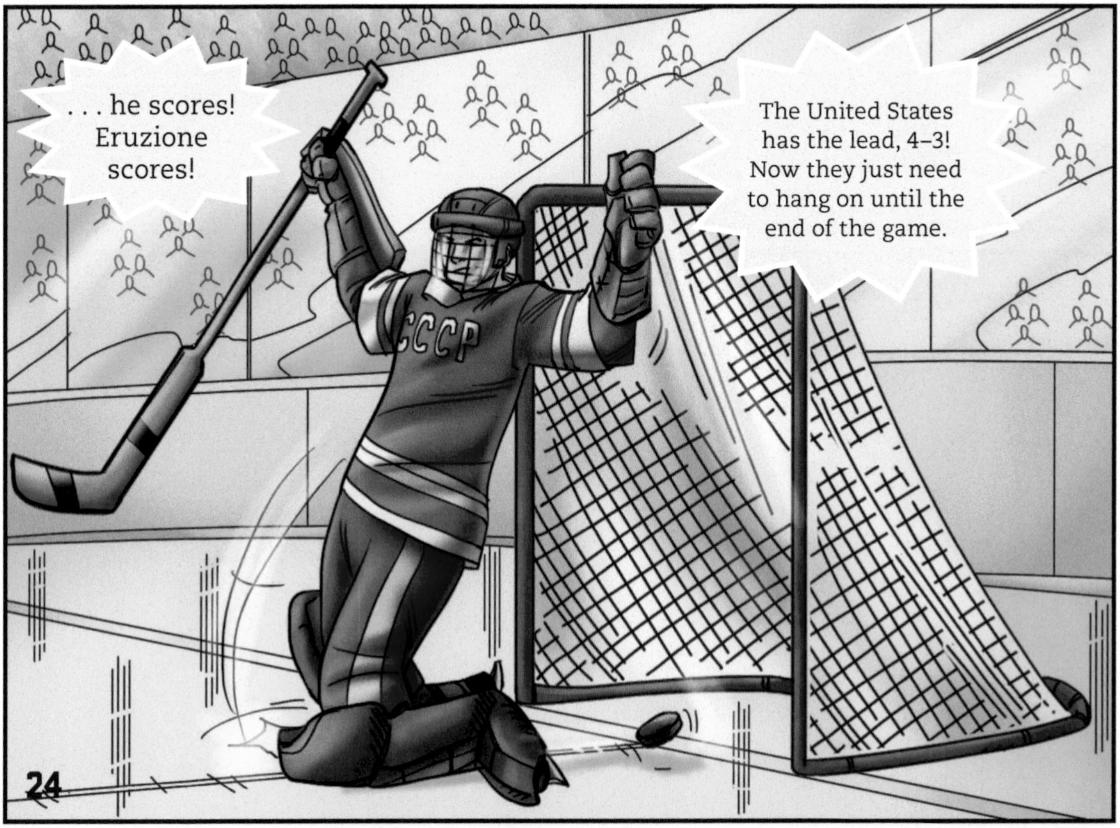
. . . he scores! Eruzione scores!
The United States has the lead, 4–3! Now they just need to hang on until the end of the game.

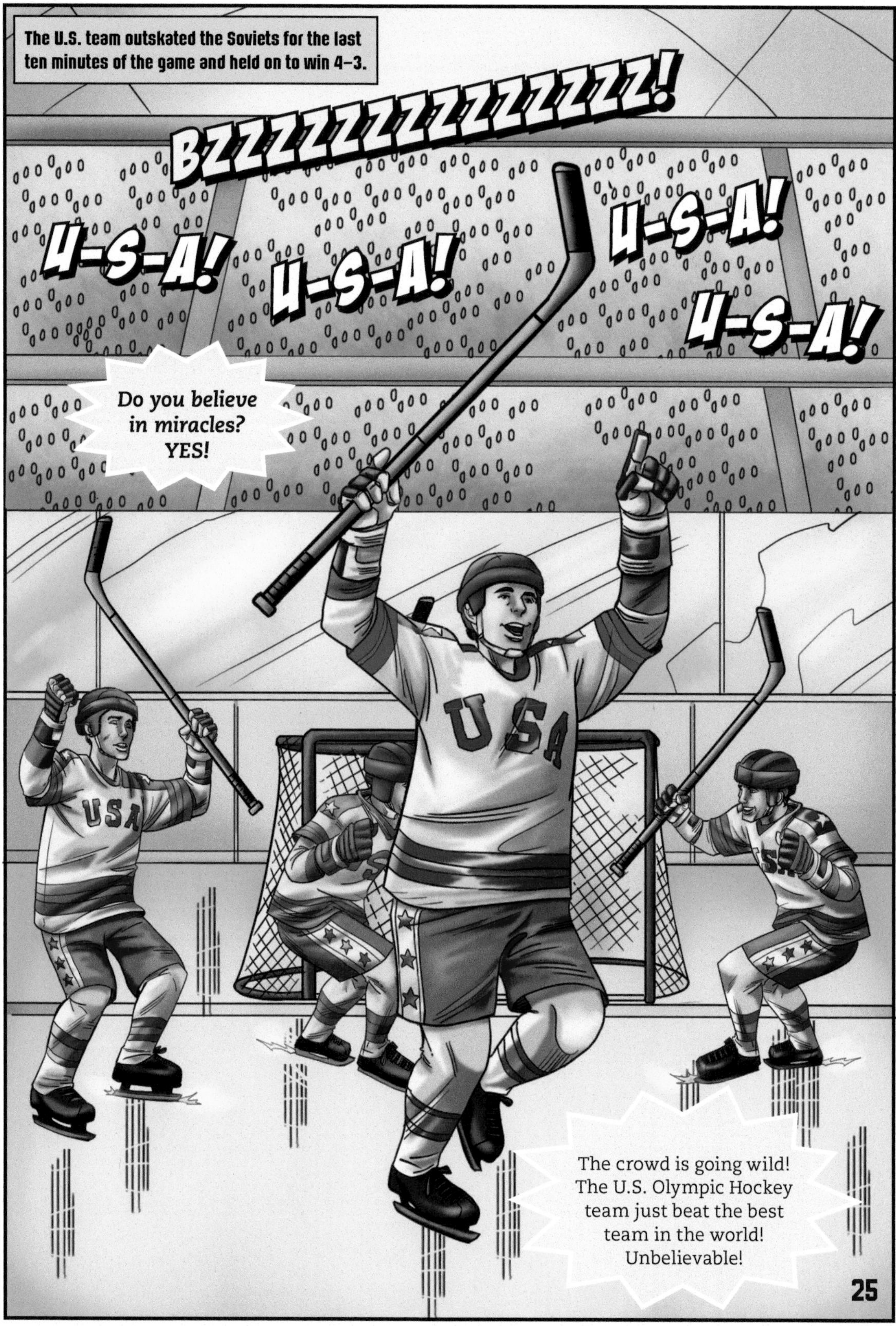
The U.S. team outskated the Soviets for the last ten minutes of the game and held on to win 4–3.
BZZZZZZZZZZZZZZZZ!
U-S-A!
U-S-A!
U-S-A!
U-S-A!
Do you believe in miracles? YES!
The crowd is going wild! The U.S. Olympic Hockey team just beat the best team in the world! Unbelievable!

WINNING IT ALL

The United States had beaten their toughest foe. But the gold medal wasn't theirs yet. They still had to face a strong Finland team.

Finland is in the power play and . . . Leinonen deflects the puck into the net. Goal!

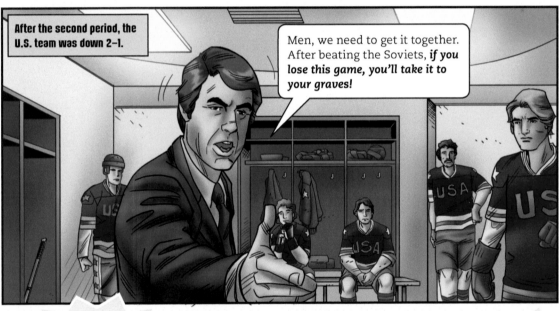

After the second period, the U.S. team was down 2–1.

Men, we need to get it together. After beating the Soviets, *if you lose this game, you'll take it to your graves!*

Brooks sure has his team fired up. They tied it at two in the second period.

McClanahan takes the pass from Johnson . . . and scores! The U.S. is now up 3–2!

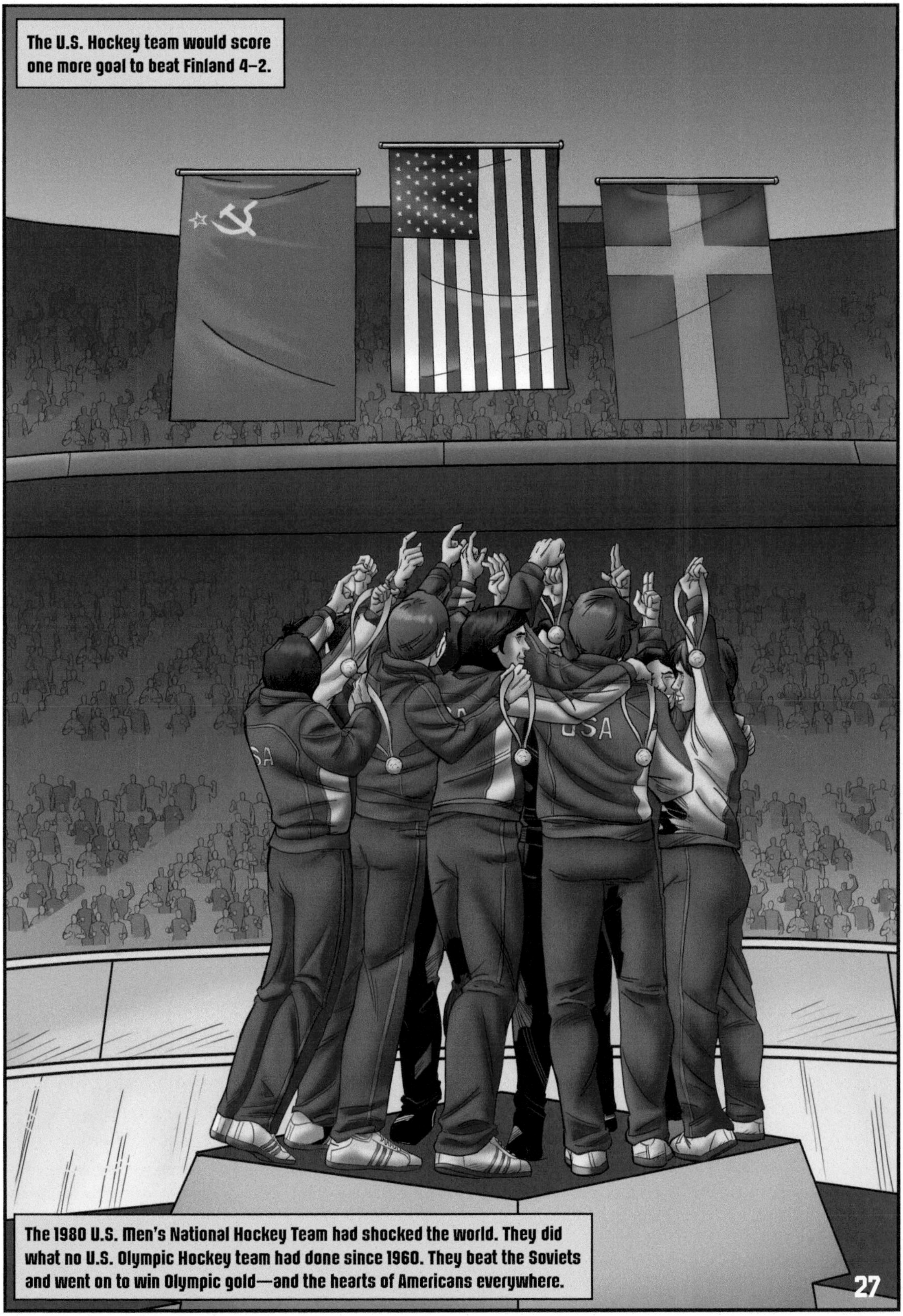
The U.S. Hockey team would score one more goal to beat Finland 4-2.
USA
USA
USA
The 1980 U.S. Men's National Hockey Team had shocked the world. They did what no U.S. Olympic Hockey team had done since 1960. They beat the Soviets and went on to win Olympic gold—and the hearts of Americans everywhere.

LIFE AFTER THE MIRACLE

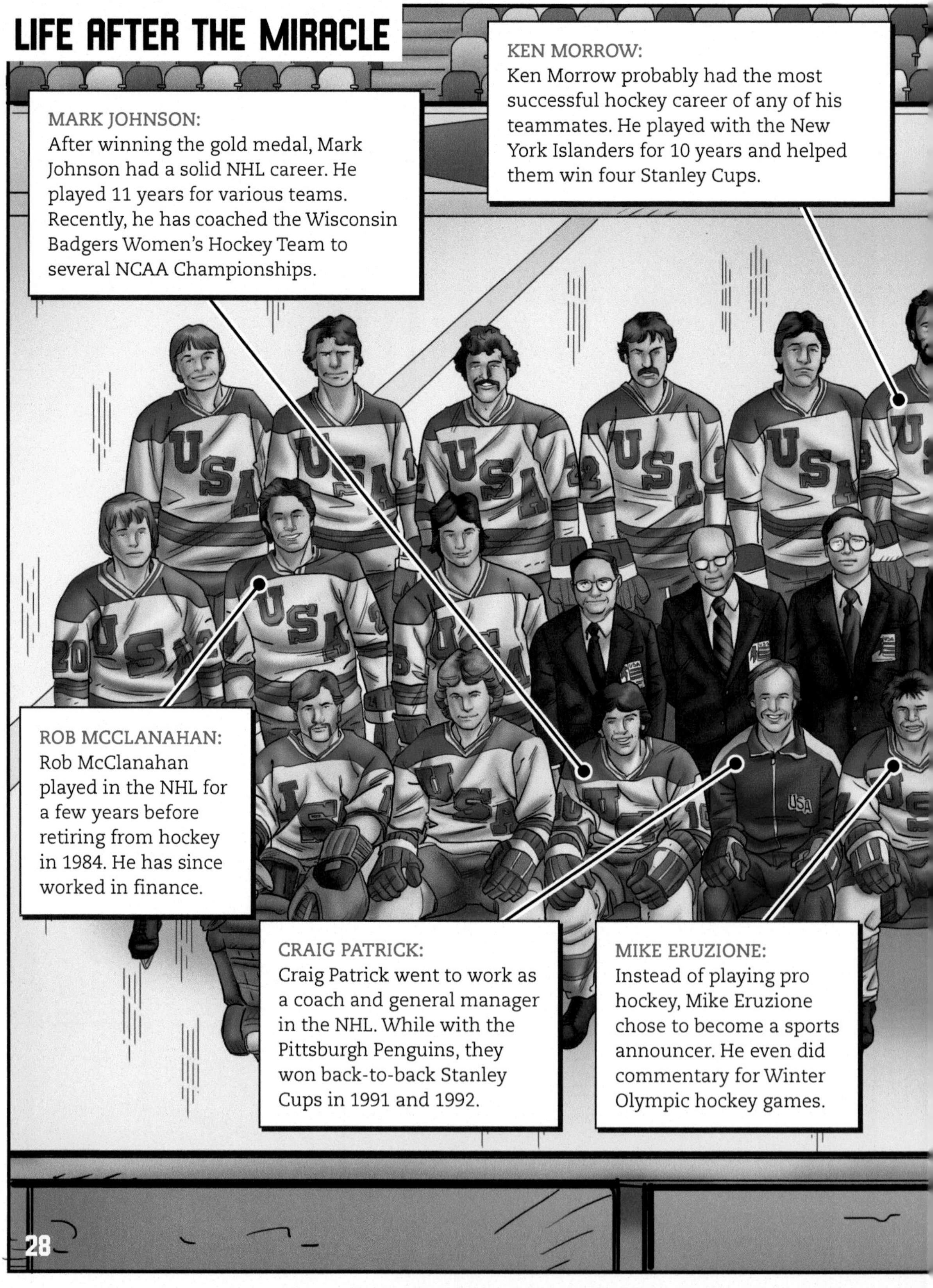
MARK JOHNSON:
After winning the gold medal, Mark Johnson had a solid NHL career. He played 11 years for various teams. Recently, he has coached the Wisconsin Badgers Women's Hockey Team to several NCAA Championships.
KEN MORROW:
Ken Morrow probably had the most successful hockey career of any of his teammates. He played with the New York Islanders for 10 years and helped them win four Stanley Cups.
ROB MCCLANAHAN:
Rob McClanahan played in the NHL for a few years before retiring from hockey in 1984. He has since worked in finance.
CRAIG PATRICK:
Craig Patrick went to work as a coach and general manager in the NHL. While with the Pittsburgh Penguins, they won back-to-back Stanley Cups in 1991 and 1992.
MIKE ERUZIONE:
Instead of playing pro hockey, Mike Eruzione chose to become a sports announcer. He even did commentary for Winter Olympic hockey games.

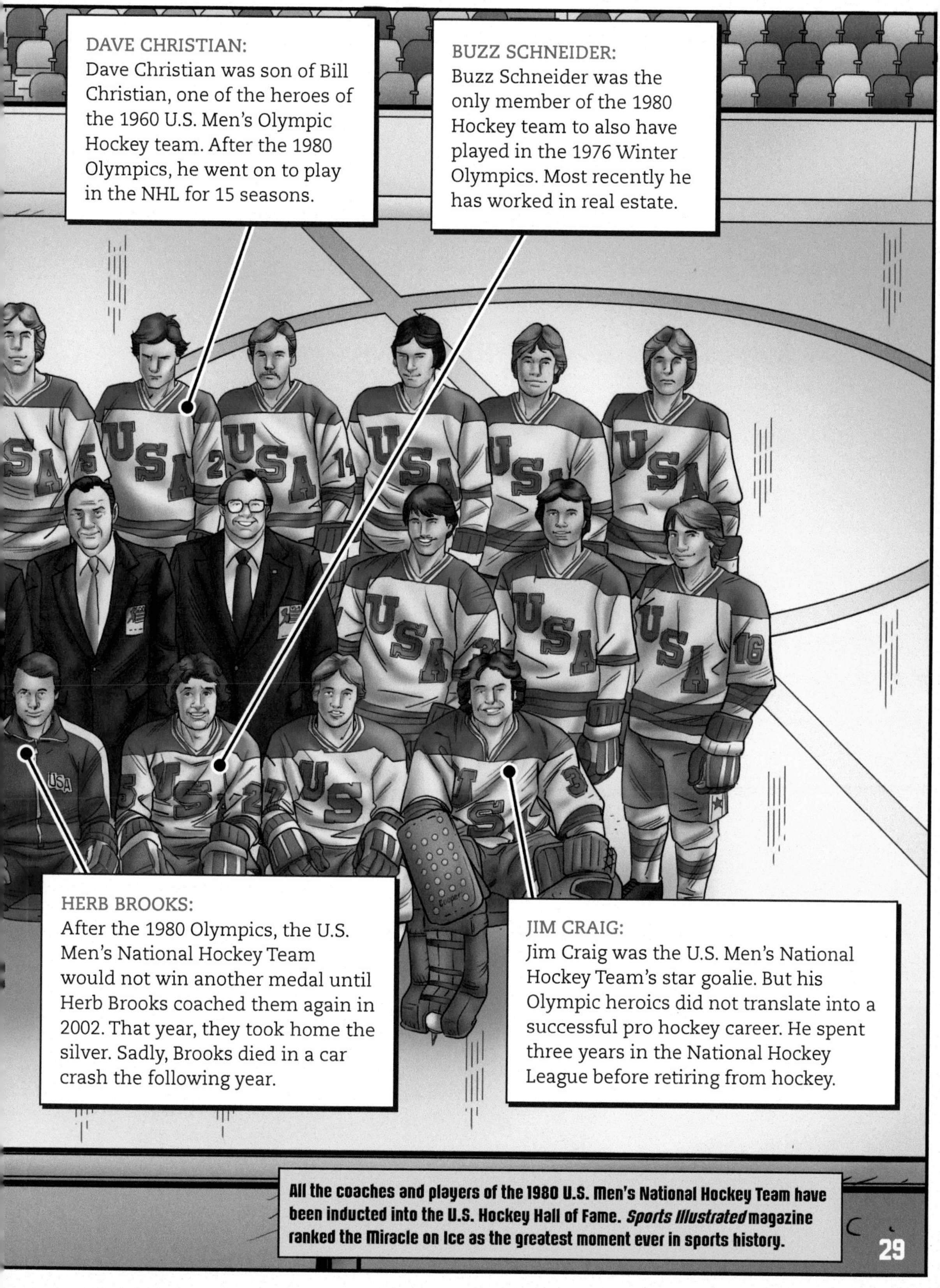
DAVE CHRISTIAN:
Dave Christian was son of Bill Christian, one of the heroes of the 1960 U.S. Men's Olympic Hockey team. After the 1980 Olympics, he went on to play in the NHL for 15 seasons.
BUZZ SCHNEIDER:
Buzz Schneider was the only member of the 1980 Hockey team to also have played in the 1976 Winter Olympics. Most recently he has worked in real estate.
HERB BROOKS:
After the 1980 Olympics, the U.S. Men's National Hockey Team would not win another medal until Herb Brooks coached them again in 2002. That year, they took home the silver. Sadly, Brooks died in a car crash the following year.
JIM CRAIG:
Jim Craig was the U.S. Men's National Hockey Team's star goalie. But his Olympic heroics did not translate into a successful pro hockey career. He spent three years in the National Hockey League before retiring from hockey.
All the coaches and players of the 1980 U.S. Men's National Hockey Team have been inducted into the U.S. Hockey Hall of Fame. *Sports Illustrated* magazine ranked the Miracle on Ice as the greatest moment ever in sports history.

GLOSSARY

amateur (AM-uh-chur)—an athlete who is not paid for playing a sport

breakaway (BRAKE-uh-way)—when a player has possession of the puck and there are no defenders other than the goalie between him and the goal

conditioning (kuhn-DISH-uhn-ing)—the act of training the body for top physical performance

contender (kuhn-TEN-dur)—someone who competes for a championship

exhibition (ek-suh-BI-shuhn)—a game or display in which someone publicly shows their skills and abilities

face-off (FAYS-off)—in hockey, when the referee drops the puck between one player from each team; the players battle for possession of the puck to start or restart play

hat trick (HAT TRIK)—when a hockey player scores three goals in one game

penalty (PEN-uhl-tee)—punishment when a player breaks the rules; the player has to sit in the penalty box for two or more minutes

period (PEER-ee-uhd)—an equal portion of playing time for an athletic game; hockey periods last 20 minutes

power play (POW-ur PLAY)—when a hockey team has a one- or two-player advantage because the other team has players in the penalty box

rebound (REE-bound)—a puck that bounces off a goalkeeper while attempting to make a save

strategy (STRAT-uh-jee)—a plan for winning a competition

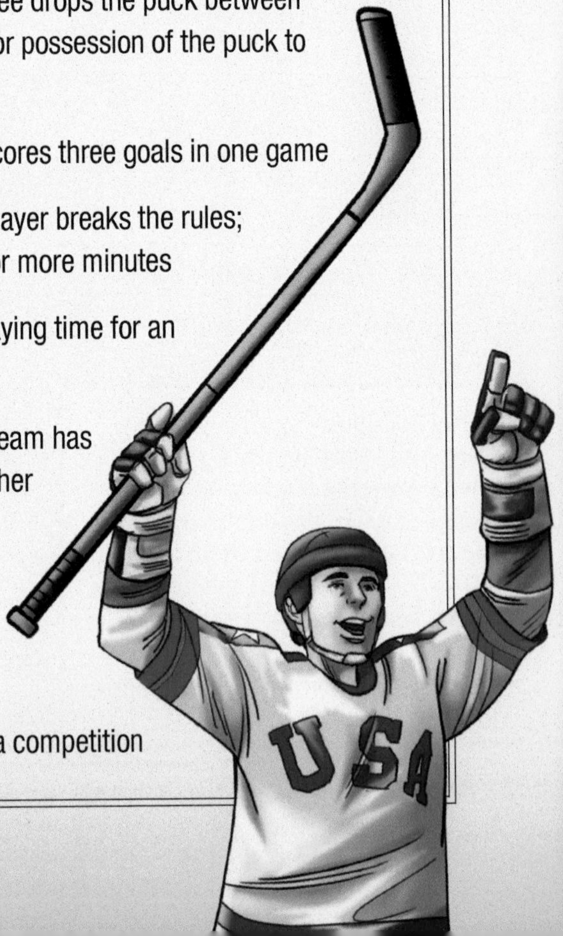
USA

READ MORE

Bradley, Michael. *Pro Hockey's Underdogs: Players and Teams Who Shocked the Hockey World.* Sports Shockers! North Mankato, Minn.: Capstone Press, 2018.

Burgan, Michael. *Miracle on Ice: How a Stunning Upset United a Country.* Captured Sports History. North Mankato, Minn.: Capstone Press, 2016.

Trusdell, Brian. *The Miracle on Ice.* Greatest Events in Sports History. Minneapolis: Abdo Publishing, 2015.

CRITICAL THINKING QUESTIONS

- Herb Brooks was the last player cut from the 1960 U.S. Men's Olympic Hockey team that won a gold medal. How might that have motivated him when preparing for the 1980 Olympics?

- In 1980 the Soviet Union was heavily favored to win the gold medal. But the U.S. Hockey team won gold by scoring just one more point than the Soviets. It was a miraculous achievement. However, if the U.S. team had lost against Finland, they wouldn't have won the gold medal. Do you think that would have made beating the Soviets any less important?

- Coach Brooks knew the U.S. team had to change its style of play to compete with teams like the Soviets. Have you ever had to change how you do something in order to succeed? Explain your answer.

INTERNET SITES

Use Facthound to find Internet sites related to this book.

Visit *www.facthound.com*

Just type in 9781543528671 and go.

 Check out projects, games and lots more at
www.capstonekids.com

INDEX